CHILDREN OF THE DEVELOPING COUNTRIES

Children of the
Developing Countries

A REPORT BY

UNICEF

Published for the United Nations Children's Fund by

THE WORLD PUBLISHING COMPANY

CLEVELAND AND NEW YORK

Published by The World Publishing Company
2231 West 110th Street, Cleveland 2, Ohio

Published simultaneously in Canada by
Nelson, Foster & Scott Ltd.

Library of Congress Catalog Card Number: 63-14805

FIRST EDITION

CONTENTS

PREFACE

The objective of the "United Nations Decade of Development," as the 1960's have been designated by the General Assembly, is a world-wide mobilization of effort to assist the low-income countries along the road toward self-sustaining economic growth and social advancement. Programs for children and youth occupy an important place in this crucial decade, for the development of the world's human resources, as represented by the rising generation, is as vital as investment in capital goods or the exploitation of natural resources.

The concern of UNICEF—the United Nations Children's Fund—in this Development Decade is to promote the improvement of the condition of children in the developing countries. The greatest improvements will be obtained if their needs are taken into consideration in planning and executing the long-range economic and social development programs now gathering pace in these countries. A considerable amount of international aid is available to these countries, including bilateral and multilateral government assistance, the assistance of voluntary agencies, private investment, and grants-in-aid made by the Fund itself.

The present report covers and briefly describes the outstanding needs of children in the developing countries, some of the policy questions involved in meeting these needs, the principal measures being taken, the opportunities for further action, and the assistance being provided by the world community. Included in the general text are summaries of the assistance UNICEF gives in various fields. A final chapter describes the organization and financing of UNICEF.

MAURICE PATE
Executive Director, United Nations Children's Fund

v

"We must prepare as well as protect the child."

CHILDREN OF THE DEVELOPING COUNTRIES

CHAPTER I

Programs for Children—
an Investment in Human Resources

Out of humanitarian motives everyone wants to do something for children. But in view of the scarcity of national and international resources for general development purposes in the poorer areas of the world, many thoughtful persons in policy-making positions question the wisdom of allocating substantial resources to programs specifically designed to meet the needs of children. Their doubts on this score are intensified by the rapid increase in child population, commonly attributed to improved health services, and the fear that even food production will not be able to keep pace. They are inclined to believe that economic development must be given priority if any lasting gains, including those of a humanitarian nature, are to be achieved.

In preparing this report, humanitarian considerations have been rather taken for granted. This is not to suggest that in the long run moral considerations are not the most important ones or that, in the words of the Declaration of the Rights of the Child, mankind owes the child anything less than "the best it has to give." What a country can do for its children, however, is limited by its economic progress, and a decision to concentrate all resources on economic development could be motivated by the highest ideals.

A question, therefore, that must be realistically faced is: "How much attention should be given to children's needs in a country's development plans?" Not only the welfare of the 500 million children now growing up in the developing countries, but the kind of preparation for life they will receive, depend on the answers given this question in different countries throughout the world. Because such a large percentage of humanity is involved, these answers cannot fail to affect the future of the whole world. To realize the extent to which they will affect its economic future, it is only necessary to recall that from the ranks of today's children must be drawn the planners, the administrators, the industrial and commercial supervisors, and the other key personnel who will chart and direct the economic affairs

1

of the coming decades; the new migrants to industrial areas whose success in acquiring job skills and in adapting to the disciplines of factory work will be of critical importance to the whole course of industrial development; and the cultivators whose willingness to adopt new agricultural techniques will, to a very large extent, govern the expansion of the world's food supply.

THE ECONOMIC BACKGROUND

Two-thirds of the world's people, including perhaps three-quarters of the world's children, live in countries that have not yet reached a level of economic and industrial development sufficient to assure their inhabitants even a minimum measure of the "freedom from want" that is one of the goals of the world community. These countries, which are located largely in the tropics and subtropics, are now trying to launch themselves on an ascending curve of self-sustaining growth. The approximately 120 countries and territories in this category are usually referred to as the "developing countries" (or alternatively as the "economically underdeveloped countries"). These are countries where steel and mechanical energy are relatively little used, where there is a shortage of efficient transportation and communications systems, and where the basic measure of a day's work is still, by and large, what a man can accomplish with his two hands and a few simple tools. In these countries, two-thirds or three-fourths of the labor force may be engaged in agriculture, but in most of them the population is not adequately fed, for agricultural productivity is extremely low. It is estimated, for example, that in Asia more than 100 man-days of labor are required on the average to bring an acre of ground to harvest as against two man-days of labor in the United States.

The use of the term "developing countries" should not obscure the fact that these countries are still developing much less rapidly than the economically advanced countries. The combined income of the developing countries, excluding Mainland China, is of the order of $175 billion (only $60 billion more than the countries of the economically advanced world spend on armaments every year). It is increasing by $5-10 billion a year. The combined national income of the developed countries is of the order of $1,000 billion and is growing each year by $40-50 billion. This is natural since development is a cumulative process. The result, however, is an increasing disparity between living standards in the low-income and high-income countries at a time when better world communications make the contrast continually more obvious. (This is true, in any event, of living standards as measured by the visible supply of consumer goods, though in some important matters, such as health and life expectancy, the developing countries are reducing the gap that separates them from the developed.) The contrast

2

in wealth between today's low-income and high-income countries is a phenomenon of the past 200 years; in earlier periods, some of today's low-income areas were the more economically advanced.

A consequence of this very unequal distribution of the world's wealth is that persons who have spent their lives in the economically advanced countries have to make a special effort to conceive of the extreme poverty that, despite the existence of a few pockets of affluence, dominates life in the developing countries. The average weekly income per head in these countries is $2 (or, say, $10 per family), a tenth or a twentieth of what it is in the economically advanced countries. With this poverty go many ills. As many as a third of the children die before they reach the age of five. Undernutrition and malnutrition affect half the population of the developing countries and more than half the children. Only half the children who survive their early years go to school, and a very small proportion receive the training or guidance they need for life in the rapidly changing world in which they are growing up.

The situation is not a static one. Many of the countries of Asia, Africa, and Latin America are now experiencing the same kind of industrial revolution that transformed the lives of the people of Europe and North America about a hundred and fifty years ago. They must do this if they are to raise their standards of living so as to provide a better life for their children. But many of the changes taking place involve difficult adjustments. This is particularly true of youths, husbands, and whole families, who migrate from the countryside and plunge into the competitive existence of industrial work and the mushrooming cities. Very few social services are available to help them acclimate to this radically new environment they find themselves in.

THE POPULATION PROBLEM

The present unprecedented growth in the world's total population is one of the major social problems of our day and aggravates many of the problems of children by the demands it places on family resources and social facilities, for example, the demand for additional places in school. Out of a world population of approximately 3 billion, 2 billion live in the developing countries as defined above. If Mainland China, about which we have relatively little information, is excluded, the population of the developing countries comes to 1,300,000,000, of whom about 500 million are children under fifteen. In these countries the general decline in death rates which has taken place in the past twenty or thirty years has not been matched by a comparable decline in birth rates. The average rate of population growth in the developing countries is higher than in the economically advanced countries, and is generally between two and three per cent per year. A world population of at least 6 billion in the year 2000 A.D. has to be planned for, and a tremendous investment will be required to meet the needs of these increased numbers. In a country where the rate of natural increase comes to 2.5 per cent per year, for example, the equivalent of 10 per cent of the national income must go into capital formation each year just to keep the standard of living from declining.

Part of the economic and social mission of the United Nations organizations, as set by the member nations in their governing bodies, is to help to raise standards of living in the developing countries. This is part of the answer to the population problem, for if economic and social development can be accelerated so that they outstrip population growth in these countries, the eventual result—granted that past trends in the industrialized countries provide any reliable basis for prediction—should be a moderation in the rate of population increase, though it is difficult to foresee how long it would take for this to come about.

Any limitation of the number of children born in the remaining years of this century depends on hundreds of millions of family decisions. One of the general effects of a rising standard of living is to help break the hold of fatalism. When people realize that it is in their power to improve the conditions under which they live and under which their children will live, a great deal of progress becomes possible. Social programs that improve the chances of the child's surviving and growing up to realize his potentials encourage parents to value smaller, better-cared-for families. It is the view of the United Nations Population Commission that each country must decide for itself whether to supplement these anticipated effects of industrialization and social development with family planning information disseminated through government channels. Several countries have adopted this course.

The spread of modern medicine has already disrupted the brutal "balance of nature" that once kept population in check. Whether or not further programs for children are undertaken, many more of the children born every year will now survive than did twenty or thirty years ago. Long-range programs for their benefit now serve largely to help them become healthier, more energetic, and better educated adults—hence to improve the quality of the next generation. Serious as the population problem is, it is no excuse for the welfare of children to be neglected.

SHORTAGE OF PERSONNEL

In the very countries commonly thought of as having too great a population for their economic good, there is usually a crying shortage of trained "personnel," meaning the technicians, supervisors, teachers, and skilled workers necessary for the growth and development of a modern society. Such

4

GHANA. Today's children are tomorrow's citizens. Survival is the first
of the child's needs, but only the first.

INDIA. Despite the existence of a few pockets of affluence, extreme poverty dominates life in the developing countries.

SIERRA LEONE. Careful planning—from the ministerial down to the village level—
is essential if programs for children are to be brought into
the mainstream of development.

THAILAND. School garden at Teachers Training College in Ubol. Using schools to teach health, nutrition, and other practical matters, in addition to academic subjects, is an example of sound planning.

personnel need, at the very least, a primary education plus some further technical or vocational training; a good part of them need a secondary education plus further study or training. A country's "personnel potential" is therefore limited by the number of children who are able to complete their primary and secondary schooling. The charts on page 6 show the main stages of attrition between birth and completion of secondary school in five countries. The contrast between the two high-income and the three low-income countries is striking and typical. In the low-income countries the large number of children born every year is reduced to a small trickle of potential personnel by the time their childhood is completed. It is these countries that suffer from a tremendous waste of human resources.

The administrator or planner approaching this problem purely from the viewpoint of the needs of the economy would first of all try to expand the present trickle of graduates of secondary and technical schools into a more substantial flow. Along these lines, the Conference of African States on Education held in Addis Ababa in May 1961 adopted a plan to double secondary school enrolment in the period 1961-6, whereas primary school enrolment was to be expanded by only 30 per cent. The administrator would also concern himself with vocational training and guidance for older children and adolescents. He might very well reach the conclusion that urban social services should be strengthened to help migrants from the rural areas acquire the habits and skills of industrial workers. Looking further ahead, he would be interested in broadening the lower steps of the personnel pyramid. He would then concern himself with the expansion of primary education. (The high proportion of children in the developing countries who start primary school but do not finish is a problem touched on in Chapter IV of this report.) Finally, he would logically find himself concerned with health services and better nutrition for the pre-school child, for ill-health and malnutrition, not only cut the numbers of children entering the primary grades, but impair their later development as well.

In this manner the administrator would be likely to arrive at the same type of over-all program for children, involving both protection and preparation for life, that has logically evolved—though in an altogether different order—from a consideration of the "rights of the child." Among these rights, the right to survival is naturally taken as the most basic, and this has led to extensive efforts to reduce infant mortality. At the end of World War II, a number of maternal and child health services in the underdeveloped countries were concentrating on midwifery. Since then there has been a movement to extend health protection to the infant and to the vulnerable weanling and pre-school child, to improve the nutrition of young children, and to bring endemic diseases under control. Day-care centers for the children of working mothers and special programs for other children who cannot re-

MAIN STAGES OF ATTRITION BETWEEN BIRTH AND COMPLETION OF SECONDARY SCHOOL IN TWO HIGH-INCOME COUNTRIES AND IN THREE LOW-INCOME COUNTRIES

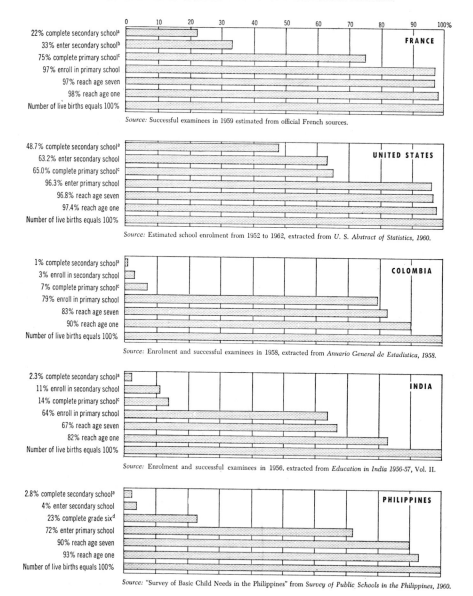

22% complete secondary school[a]
33% enter secondary school[b]
75% complete primary school[c]
97% enroll in primary school
97% reach age seven
98% reach age one
Number of live births equals 100%

FRANCE

Source: Successful examinees in 1959 estimated from official French sources.

48.7% complete secondary school[a]
63.2% enter secondary school
65.0% complete primary school[c]
96.3% enter primary school
96.8% reach age seven
97.4% reach age one
Number of live births equals 100%

UNITED STATES

Source: Estimated school enrolment from 1952 to 1962, extracted from *U. S. Abstract of Statistics, 1960.*

1% complete secondary school[a]
3% enroll in secondary school
7% complete primary school[c]
79% enroll in primary school
83% reach age seven
90% reach age one
Number of live births equals 100%

COLOMBIA

Source: Enrolment and successful examinees in 1958, extracted from *Anuario General de Estadística, 1958.*

2.3% complete secondary school[a]
11% enroll in secondary school
14% complete primary school[c]
64% enroll in primary school
67% reach age seven
82% reach age one
Number of live births equals 100%

INDIA

Source: Enrolment and successful examinees in 1956, extracted from *Education in India 1956-57*, Vol. II.

2.8% complete secondary school[a]
4% enter secondary school
23% complete grade six[d]
72% enter primary school
90% reach age seven
93% reach age one
Number of live births equals 100%

PHILIPPINES

Source: "Survey of Basic Child Needs in the Philippines" from *Survey of Public Schools in the Philippines, 1960.*

[a] Complete twelve years of school.
[b] Secondary school includes lycées, collèges techniques, and cours complémentaires.
[c] Complete eight years of school.
[d] Complete six years of school.

ceive the full care they need in the home are measures that are being undertaken to fulfil the child's right to protection during his tender years. Though about half the children of primary school age in the developing countries still do not attend school, progress has been made toward the goal of universal primary education as a first step toward fulfilling the child's general right to "an education which will . . . enable him on a basis of equal opportunity to develop his abilities . . . and to become a useful member of society."

Thus the approach of the economist concerned over shortages of trained personnel and that of the person concerned with the rights of the child as an individual tend, in the long run, to meet on a common ground of action. Philosophically, too, they are not so opposed as they might seem, for the rights of the child are very incompletely served by "saving a life" during infancy or early childhood but never developing his potentials, the potential for satisfying work included.

THE NEED FOR BALANCED ECONOMIC
AND SOCIAL DEVELOPMENT

Programs to improve the condition of children are social development programs. The final object of economic development and of social development is the same: a better life. Economic development contributes to this indirectly by providing the means. Social programs—health, education, and social welfare services, among others—contribute to this end directly by helping people make the best use of the means available to improve their lives. Genuine progress—that is to say, progress measurable in human terms —can best be ensured by balanced economic and social development. In any particular country, this balance will be a delicate task to maintain. There is no need to maintain it too precisely, for the tensions arising from a certain imbalance may serve as a spur to development efforts. But too great an imbalance will impede economic and social development alike.

The problem is simplified by the fact that there are many areas—including a great many affecting the needs of children—where action is required for both economic and social reasons. Education is a good example. A distinguished economist advised the Conference of African States on Education, referred to above, that, from the point of view of economic development alone, the first target of the countries south of the Sahara might well be, in terms of the respective age groups, 50 per cent enrolment in primary school, 5 per cent in secondary school, and 0.5 per cent in universities, with many other graduates of primary and secondary school going on to technical training. This first target would cost about 2 per cent of the national income of these countries. The next target proposed, to double these enrolments, would cost 4 per cent of the national income. Even this is considerably below the level suggested as a final goal by social considerations—up to 8 per cent of the national income as interpreted by some developed countries, the USSR for example—but it is considerably above current average performance.

The Economic and Social Council and the General Assembly of the United Nations have recommended that the developing countries give a high priority to programs from which both economic and social benefits can be immediately derived.

Even outside those areas where common programs of action may be framed, there are important mutual relationships between economic and social development efforts. Economic development and a rising standard of living are, in general, the best social medicine. It would, however, be erroneous to conclude from this proposition that there is no need to give special attention to social problems. It would be false, for example, to assume that if the income of a cultivator is raised by an increased production of cash crops, he will necessarily buy and know how to use better food for the nourishment of his family. As a matter of fact, people changing from a subsistence to a money economy tend to spend a large part of their income on "unproductive" items.

On the other hand, economic development may exacerbate certain social problems. Thus industrialization, in its earlier stages at least, tends to encourage the growth of urban slums; the slum environment in turn creates difficult problems of social adjustment and tends to depress the health and productivity of labor.

More important to emphasize, because it is the least recognized aspect of their mutual relations, is the fact that social programs may, and frequently do, speed the process of economic development.

Industry is nourished by migrants from rural areas who flock to the cities looking for work. Industry will benefit from any social programs that help these people adjust to urban life and that protect their health and nutrition. It will also benefit from any vocational training and guidance programs that can be carried out on their behalf.

The task of *agriculture* is to increase food production so that the growing proportion of the population engaged in industry may be adequately nourished. Here again the social contribution to development is an essential one. Increased agricultural production depends on substantial technical innovations, such as irrigation, multiple cropping, the use of chemical fertilizers. The spread of such improved agricultural techniques ultimately depends on the decisions and actions of millions of individual cultivators and can be greatly facilitated by the education of rural populations, as was strikingly illustrated by Denmark in the 19th century and Japan in the 20th. In fact, a clear correlation has been noticed between the rate of literacy in different countries and their use of chemical fertilizers. Certain disease control campaigns contribute directly to agricultural development: campaigns against malaria, for example, since the season when outbreaks of malaria are most widespread and severe is usually the season of peak agricultural work.

Nutrition programs also have far-reaching economic implications. Widespread nutrition education and the planned development of agricultural production along lines needed to fulfil the nutritional needs of the population can help to keep the balance between supply and demand from being badly upset by the changing pattern of demand for various foods that usually accompanies a rising standard of living.

INVESTMENT IN HUMAN RESOURCES

The need for an intensive investment of long-term development capital in the present decade in order to prepare an adequate base for future economic development is generally agreed to, both by the developing countries and the countries that are giving them financial assistance. This agreement is frequently accompanied by an unspoken assumption that the only proper objects of such an intensive investment effort are capital goods of a material nature: irrigation works, roads, railways, ports, factories, and so forth. Little account is generally taken of the importance of investing in the rising generation itself, the generation that must acquire the skills, attitudes, and knowledge to use these capital goods efficiently.

In the developing countries, children generally join the labor force at the age of twelve, some indeed at an earlier age. Up to that time they have to be considered as an economic liability. Yet within a few years they will be the basis of the economy of these countries. Hence has come the concept of investment in children, involving an input of resources up to about the age of twelve and returns from then on. This concept is elaborated here, not as a Machiavellian justification for programs whose urgency on ethical grounds alone is unquestionable, but to provoke examination of an important practical question: whether children are entitled only to a share of those resources that the world budgets for "good works and charity," or whether both the long-range interests of children and the cause of economic advancement will not be better served by considering the needs of children in planning the use of the much greater resources that must of necessity be devoted to general development.

If all that must be done for a child before he is old enough to provide for himself is regarded purely in terms of its economic cost, it is obvious that the return on this investment will be zero if the child dies before he reaches working age. The return will be incomplete if the productive years of his

9

life are short or are spent in poor health. The expectation of working life is now being lengthened rapidly in the developing countries, but in many of them it does not yet extend to the normal age of retirement. For example, a boy of 15 in India or Brazil can expect, on the average, to live only to the age of 55, whereas in the economically advanced countries he can expect to reach the age of 65 or more.

Expectation of life, once adulthood is reached, depends not only on what happens to the individual as an adult, but also on the care he has had as a child. Severe malnutrition in childhood leaves permanent injuries: protein deficiency can result in permanent damage to the liver; vitamin A deficiency, to the eyes. Diseases such as trachoma or yaws of the bone leave the child victim handicapped for the rest of his life. Some disabling infections that declare themselves later are acquired in childhood—tuberculosis and leprosy, for example. The degree of energy and alertness an adult can bring to his tasks depends partly on his current food consumption and the current state of his health; the extent to which it also depends on factors associated with his early childhood has not yet been satisfactorily established. From what we know, however, it seems highly probable that the cost of lowered vitality having its origin in childhood sickness and malnutrition exceeds that of the overt diseases and handicaps originating in childhood.

Because of high child mortality, the relatively short expectation of life once working age has been reached, and the low level of vitality at which much of the working population functions, the developing countries receive at present a very low rate of return on the investment that the care of their children represents. Programs to improve the health and nutrition of children represent an additional immediate investment, but one that tends within a generation to raise the net rate of return on a country's investment in human resources.

It has been calculated that in the economically advanced countries a better education will bring a return to the individual and society many times greater than its cost. In the developing countries, where progress in almost all fields is being retarded by severe shortages of qualified personnel, the proportionate returns from investment in education could be even higher. Unfortunately the developing countries are unable to exploit this investment opportunity sufficiently. Because of the age distribution of the population, the economic strain on the income-earning population is severe. In a typical developing country, there are about 70 children to every 100 productive adults, as against 50 to every 100 productive adults in the economically advanced countries. Thus the developing countries, which are short of capital, have a relatively large input; yet, because they cannot invest enough to meet the needs of their children at all adequately, they get a smaller return.

In recent years the economically advanced countries have shown an increased willingness to help the developing countries meet their needs for development capital. One area in which such assistance is badly needed— and certainly one of the areas in which it might be most profitably employed —is investment in human resources.

Internal Resources of the Developing Countries.   The annual national incomes of the developing countries, exclusive of Mainland China, total about $175 billion a year—about one-sixth of the combined income of the economically advanced countries, as we have seen. While the situation varies greatly among the developing countries, it is not too misleading to think of education getting about 3 per cent of the national income, health 1 per cent, and other social services 1 per cent. Current expenditures for these purposes may, therefore, total as much as $8 or $9 billion annually, but they are still insufficient to provide schooling for more than half the children of these countries or to bring health services to more than a small fraction of them.

Apart from these recurring expenditures, which will gradually increase and which, in some cases, may be spent more effectively in the future, the developing countries are also making capital or development expenditures, often under a separate budget. Total new investment, mostly for economic development, in these countries is now running to the equivalent of $10 billion per year. According to unofficial estimates, about twice that amount is needed if self-sustaining economic growth is to be achieved. No analysis is available of how much of these capital or development expenditures have any relation to programs particularly benefiting children.

Resources from Outside the Developing Countries.   The net flow of public economic assistance and long-term capital from the developed to the developing countries has been steadily increasing in recent years. The outflow from the private enterprise countries of the developed world rose from $5.2 billion in 1959 to $6 billion in 1960 and reached a new high of $7.2 billion in 1961, originating as follows:

Government grants	$3,520 million
Government loans	2,626 million
Private investment	1,050 million
	$7,196 million

Source: International Flow of Long-term Capital and Official Donations, 1959-1961 (United Nations document A/5195, October 1962).

Credits and grants extended by the centrally-planned economies (the USSR, Eastern Europe, etc.) to the low-income countries came to about $900 million in 1961. Included under government grants and loans were about $400 million of multilateral assistance channeled through the United Nations system. Not included is the flow of surplus foods from the high-income to the low-income countries, which in recent years has amounted to about the equivalent of $1.5 billion a year and is expected to increase.

There appear to be good prospects that the total flow of aid will continue to grow—and that it may be supplemented by efforts to stabilize the prices of the export commodities on which the developing countries depend for their own foreign exchange earnings. The United Nations General Assembly of 1960 "expressed the hope that the flow of international assistance and capital should be increased substantially so as to reach as soon as possible approximately 1 per cent of the combined national incomes of the economically advanced countries"—a target that would come to at least $12 billion a year by the mid-1960's.

The proportion of the present flow of international resources devoted specifically to children is minute, though some of the government-to-government grants go to strengthen education and health services, and some of the surplus foods shipped abroad are used in child feeding projects. A somewhat greater proportion of these total resources is available for other programs that could be of considerable benefit to children if their special needs were taken into account and planned for. The resources that might figure in such programs include, not only the loans and grants extended by individual countries and groups of countries (the European Economic Community, the Colombo Plan, the Scandinavian group, etc.), but some of the international flow of private capital: for example, that invested in food processing plants.

At present, there is no known assessment of the proportion of these resources going either directly or indirectly to investments in human resources rather than to investments in capital hardware. A statistical breakdown along these lines, even if it could be made, would not be very valuable in itself. It would be tremendously useful, however, to have the value of human investment regularly considered in the planning of development programs, with perhaps some over-all review of whether the proportion going into it is sufficient.

United Nations Assistance. A small fraction of the total flow of resources from the outside, about $400 million a year, is channeled through the United Nations and the Specialized Agencies. A substantial part of this consists of net World Bank loans after deducting repayments. United Nations Technical Assistance expenditures and the training and pre-investment expenditures of the Special Fund account for most of the rest. Many of these projects will be of indirect benefit to children, among others. But only the $40 million a year at the disposal of the United Nations Children's Fund is specifically earmarked for programs to improve the condition of children.

Various voluntary agencies, many of them associated with the United Nations in a consultative status, assist projects for children in the developing countries; indeed, their total expenditures for this purpose far outstrip UNICEF's.

The $40 million a year that UNICEF allocates is not very much money in the present-day context of international assistance. Hence one of UNICEF's main objectives is to use its resources to prepare the way for larger programs under national or international auspices. The UNICEF Executive Board is progressively reorienting the Fund's pattern of aid in this direction.

UNICEF pursues this objective by allocating funds to train local personnel for services benefiting children—health workers, nutrition workers, food technologists, teachers, social workers, and administrators. It also pursues this objective through its support of field projects to work out and demonstrate measures that can be taken up on a larger scale by national ministries (disease control and social welfare projects, for example), by private industry (the commercial production of high-protein foods), or by local agencies and people (community development). These field projects also serve as "practice areas" where personnel in training may complement their theoretical instruction.

UNICEF also makes some grants to projects with national coverage designed to solve problems of particular importance to children: projects to strengthen maternal and child health services on a nation-wide level, for example. Such projects, of course, are costly.

Demonstration projects, too, must be sizable if they are to stimulate large-scale efforts. A field project needs to be large enough to get the necessary long-term work well under way, since the capacity for growth increases with local experience in planning and executing programs. It must be large enough to provide field training for a considerable number of national personnel. To influence national policy, it must be of sufficient scope and impact to command the government's attention at policy-making or cabinet level. This means, generally, that the work should cover one or more district-level administrative units. According to the country, such units will have a population ranging from several hundred thousand to one or two million people. To be effective, UNICEF should be assisting more projects of this magnitude, and it is seeking increased contributions to make this assistance possible.

NATIONAL PLANNING AND THE NEEDS OF CHILDREN

Responsibility for meeting the various needs of children is normally divided among the appropriate functional services of a given country—the health

13

ministry being responsible for maternal and child health services; the ministry of education for schooling; the ministry of social welfare for special social services for children, the operation of day-care and residential institutions; and so on. Apart from education, most children's needs can be met only through services for the whole community. Carrying out such services along functional lines is usually the most efficient procedure. Programs such as the control of endemic diseases, the development of food production, and social services to keep the family unit intact, while essential to the well-being of the child, must of necessity be run as community-wide projects. Moreover, many of the child's needs are inseparable from those of his family and community. In any event it would be philosophically unsound to regard the child as an isolated individual rather than as an integral part of his family and community.

There are, however, many important problems affecting children that cannot be adequately handled by functional ministries working separately. Often the lack of coordinated planning among the various services dealing with the needs of children makes it impossible for them to execute a coherent child-development program. There are, indeed, instances where children fail to benefit from some existing services because they have not been reached by a service administered by another department. In some countries, for example, incomplete registration of births, associated perhaps with a high rate of illegitimacy, deprives a considerable number of children of important rights and social benefits to which they would otherwise be entitled under law.

Even a limited program to meet one of the particular needs of a country's children frequently tends to cut across departmental lines and involve the work of several agencies. Thus, the nutrition of children in a given country cannot be improved without efforts on the part of the agriculture department to increase production of the required foodstuffs and efforts on the part of the health department to teach the essentials of nutrition to pregnant women and to the mothers of young children. Sometimes the same field workers can carry out dual assignments: for example, agricultural extension agents can promote better nutrition among agricultural families while showing them how to raise their living standards in other respects through increased production of cash crops. The education department will be brought into the picture when it is desirable to include nutrition education in the school curriculum, and it must reach agreement with the health department, which is responsible for the nutrition education of the mother and pre-school child, on what is to be recommended.

The various ills of children—those, for example, resulting from poverty, ignorance, sickness, malnutrition, and (particularly in the urban slums) the breakdown of family life—are closely interrelated. Each is part cause and

14

part effect of the others. Thus they are correctly described as a vicious circle. But this interrelationship also means that improving the condition of children in regard to any of these particulars will tend to strengthen efforts being carried out on their behalf in other areas as well. Greatest returns will be obtained from investment in children if there is a unified advance along all sectors pertaining to their needs.

It is easiest to demonstrate the force of this principle by showing what tends to happen otherwise. Thus, beyond a certain point, it will do little good to devote more resources to conventional health services if major nutritional problems remain unsolved. In turn, it may be impossible to advance very far in the field of nutrition without coming to grips with the problem of ignorance: many potential food sources in the developing countries are left untouched because of prejudice or lack of knowledge. Malnutrition, on the other hand, seems to be one of the principal reasons why so many children make little progress in school. And there is a limit to the progress that can be made in any of the fields where development is needed without providing the child with a better preparation for life through good schooling.

It is clear, therefore, that some kind of inter-ministerial arrangements are needed at the center of each government—bringing together the departments and agencies charged with education, health, agriculture, social welfare, finance, planning, and community development—to work out plans in areas where joint action is required to meet the needs of children and to review the progress of these plans. What is usually not needed at the present time is a new administrative hierarchy, and certainly there should be no duplication of existing administrative machinery. One of the greatest obstacles faced by the developing countries in carrying out new programs or extending existing ones, an obstacle seeming to rank with the shortage of money, is the scarcity of trained administrative talent. Under a weak administrative system, every professional leader with any initiative is likely to believe that he can develop an efficient service only if it is separate and under his own control. Where administrative talent is in short supply, however, proliferation of services is wasteful—especially when the creators of these services have handed them on to persons of less outstanding ability.

Encouraging, in this connection, is the tendency already evident in the developing countries to use existing administrative machinery for a number of different but related functions. For example, India's community development and extension program—which was itself organized around an older administrative structure, that of the district administrators in charge of justice and tax collections—serves to promote, not only community public works, but agricultural and home economics extension, adult literacy, health services, and health and nutrition education. In the organization of health services, there is a trend away from separate campaigns against individual diseases and toward integrated networks of district health offices and local health centers, both discharging multiple responsibilities. Primary schools are being used for health and nutrition education, to promote home gardening, and to teach adults to read and write. Thus each of these services reaching into local villages may be used as a channel for a number of related efforts to help rural people improve their standard of living and provide their children with a better start in life—a possibility doubly valuable since so many villages are reached by only one of these services, if they are fortunate enough to be reached by any.

Given the possibility of this kind of administrative flexibility, much can be done to meet some of the most important needs of children, provided these needs are taken account of in the broad economic and social development plans that are now being widely used to guide national efforts in the developing countries. For example, to gear agricultural development to the nutritional needs of a country's population, including the special needs of weanling and pre-school children, may require the collection and analysis of new data, and some of the personnel in the department of agriculture may have to receive additional training. Certainly, additional thought and planning will be needed. But the execution of the program in the field will cost little more in money or manpower than the execution of a development program aimed solely at increased agricultural production *per se*.

Similarly, to use the school system to teach the elements of health, nutrition, and other practical matters, in addition to academic subjects, will require an important policy decision on the part of the government; it may also add to the cost of training teachers. In terms of the money needed for the school system's actual day-to-day operations, it will cost relatively little, however. With these considerations in mind, the UNICEF Executive Board in June 1961 recommended that programs for children should be integrated with larger economic and social development plans wherever possible, and this recommendation was subsequently endorsed by the Economic and Social Council and the General Assembly of the United Nations.

In many countries the time appears to be ripe to assess the extent to which various programs affecting children support and complement one another and how more effective plans might be made where they are needed. Sometimes new field surveys may be needed to fill in gaps in the information available on the needs of children and the resources available to meet these needs. But a great deal of the work of assessment and planning can be based on existing data and information.

In 1961 the governments of 22 developing countries submitted their views and observations on the needs of children to UNICEF. These reports ranged from short resumés to detailed studies, and in some cases involved a preliminary assessment of the kind described above. They were incorporated into a preliminary inquiry into the needs of children, which the Executive Director presented, along with special reports by the ILO, FAO, WHO, UNESCO, and the United Nations Bureau of Social Affairs, to the UNICEF Executive Board in June 1961.*

This inquiry revealed the importance of a more careful examination of how the needs of children might best be met on a country-by-country basis. The Executive Board accordingly decided that it was ready to make grants to help countries initiate the work of assessment and programming. The Board also noted that many developing countries placed a high priority on some of the needs of children not previously covered by UNICEF assistance. Consequently it decided to broaden the range of UNICEF aid so that the Fund could assist countries in meeting whatever were recognized to be the major needs of their children—whether these involved projects relating to health, nutrition, education, vocational training and guidance, or broad social services. The other United Nations agencies contributing to the inquiry into the needs of children also announced their readiness to give technical advice and assistance in their respective fields, both in regard to assessment and planning and in regard to new programs of assistance that might be decided on.

The subsequent chapters of this report describe some of the serious problems affecting the children of the developing countries and what is being done about them. The more promising possibilities of future action are touched on, and the role being played by UNICEF and the other members of the United Nations family in various fields of aid is described. These chapters do not constitute a complete review of the needs of children in the developing countries. Possibilities of action have had some influence on the choice of topics.

Inadequate housing, for example, is a very important social problem and one that affects the welfare of children deeply; but, because it is not generally approached as a children's problem, it is touched on in this report only as it relates to environmental sanitation and community development. Clothing certainly has an important bearing on the needs of children. Wearing shoes, for example, reduces the likelihood of parasitic infestation. The child must have socially acceptable clothes to be admitted to school. But, apart from institutions, the kind of clothes children wear is largely determined by fashion and family income.

---

* *The Needs of Children,* ed. Georges Sicault (New York: Free Press of Glencoe, 1963).

Mental health problems have not been given the separate treatment they might deserve because the shortage of personnel skilled in diagnosis and treatment makes the situation hard to assess in the various developing countries and limits the possibilities of special mental health programs. Preventive measures on a group basis, as carried out through social services, community development programs, and the school system, seem to offer the most promising possibilities of action at the present time.

For quite a different reason the child's spiritual needs are not considered in this report. The United Nations Children's Fund is pledged to aid children of all faiths and creeds, and it would be improper for UNICEF to discuss questions pertaining in any way to religious or ideological education. There is, however, a common objective for the child's ethical development that all the members of the United Nations have agreed on, and which is embodied in the Declaration of the Rights of the Child: "He shall be brought up in a spirit of understanding, tolerance, friendship among peoples, peace and universal brotherhood, and in full consciousness that his energy and talents should be devoted to the service of his fellow men." If this principle were forgotten, there would be little point in providing the child with a better practical preparation for life, for world peace is the condition that the future of mankind depends on.

The general condition of children in the developing countries may at times appear so grim that efforts to alleviate their plight on any significant scale may appear hopeless. The answer to this will appear in detail in the following chapters. Some work is being done, and many valuable results have already been achieved. Of even greater importance is the fact that much more could be done, even without greatly increasing the over-all magnitude of international assistance, if children were accorded their due place in every country's planning for its future.

CHAPTER II

Health

Wʜɪʟᴇ ɢʀᴇᴀᴛᴇʀ ᴘʀᴏɢʀᴇss has, in recent decades, been made in the field
of health than in any other related to the needs of children, health conditions in the less developed countries are still poor. In most of the rural areas
of the tropics and subtropics, where for centuries poverty, ignorance, and
disease have gone hand-in-hand, medical services are still rudimentary.
Minimum sanitary facilities that persons in the economically developed
countries take for granted, a reliable supply of safe drinking water and
arrangements for the safe disposal of human wastes, are frequently non-
existent. Family diets generally provide less than the accepted minimum
allowances of protective foods necessary to maintain health and fight off
disease. For the poorer classes in the large cities and in the shanty-towns
surrounding these cities, health conditions may be even worse, for intense
overcrowding facilitates the spread of all infectious diseases.

Where such conditions prevail, children are the principal sufferers, for
among human beings, as among all higher animals, the most immature
organism is the most vulnerable, and the highest mortality rates prevail
among the youngest groups of children. Proper prenatal care and competent
obstetrical assistance at birth are the first of the child's health needs. Yet,
not more than one out of four of the 80 million or more births every year
in the less developed countries is assisted by so much as a trained midwife.
Maternal mortality in the less developed countries that are able to furnish
statistics in this regard is 5 to 10 times as high as it is in the economically
advanced countries, and no statistics are available for many areas where
maternal mortality is suspected of being much higher.

Infant mortality (deaths per thousand live births during the first year)
is regarded as a sensitive index of child health in a community. In the
economically advanced countries infant mortality rates range from about
15 at the best to about 50 at the worst. Again, reliable statistics are lacking
for precisely those areas where the situation is suspected of being the worst,
but the available data reveal infant mortality to be as high as 300 or 400 in
some African and Asian communities. Certainly, in the world at large,

infant mortality rates of well over 100 are still the rule rather than the exception. Infantile diarrheas, dysenteries, and other diseases related to unhygienic conditions are a principal cause of infant mortality. Furthermore, infants, like older children, are susceptible not only to childhood diseases, but to most of the infectious diseases that threaten adults. Some diseases that have to all intents and purposes been wiped out in a good part of the world, smallpox for example, still contribute significantly to infant and child mortality in certain regions.

After infancy, the years one through four are the most vulnerable period of childhood. In countries where high health standards have been achieved, mortality among children of this age, the so-called "toddler and pre-school group," has declined dramatically in the last fifty years and now runs to about one per thousand per year, or less. In the less developed countries, mortality among children of this age is typically 40 times as high. In part this is owing to the prevalence of common intestinal and respiratory diseases and the communicable diseases of childhood, diseases whose incidence has been sharply cut in the developed countries through sanitation and immunization. Undernutrition and malnutrition following weaning contribute greatly to mortality in this age group. Children of this age are also susceptible to various endemic diseases still widespread in the tropics and subtropics, such as malaria, trachoma, and bilharziasis, which are discussed later in this chapter. Diarrheas and parasitic infestations are an important cause of sickness among young children and are relatively difficult to deal with since their control depends on measures that may take a considerable time to carry out: better nutrition, improved environmental sanitation, and widespread health education.

Children who survive to school age, having surmounted the hazards of infancy and early childhood, represent a select population, and mortality rates drop sharply from the age of five on. But sickness is still common among school-age children, and health has an important effect on school attendance and on the quality of the child's achievement in school. In most of the developing countries the majority of children are at work by the age of twelve or fourteen. Older children and adolescents need special health protection in some of the occupations open to them—a protection few of them as yet receive.

PRESENT EXTENT OF HEALTH SERVICES

One rough indicator of the extent of health services in different areas is the number of inhabitants per physician.

There is no developing country here listed that does not need to double the number of its physicians, and some need to do very much more than

INHABITANTS PER PHYSICIAN

(Selected Countries)[a]

AFRICA		ASIA	
Niger	103,000	Viet-Nam	29,000
Nigeria	32,000	Burma	15,000
Cameroun	30,000	Pakistan	8,000
Ghana	21,000	Iraq	5,600
United Arab Republic	2,600	India	2,400
		Japan	930
AMERICAS		**EUROPE**	
Guatemala	6,400	Sweden[b]	1,100
Brazil	2,100	France[b]	930
Peru	2,100	Germany, Fed. Rep.[b]	730
Canada	900	Italy[b]	690
United States	780	USSR	310

[a]Annual Epidemiological and Vital Statistics 1959 (Geneva: WHO, 1962; pp. 651-660).
[b]Annual Epidemiological and Vital Statistics 1958 (Geneva: WHO, 1961; pp. 707-715).

this. The situation in the rural areas is much worse than even these figures suggest, for physicians (like other highly trained personnel) tend to remain in the cities, since the unfulfilled demand for their services in urban areas, where the pay is generally better, leaves little surplus for the rural areas. In Peru, for example, there is one physician for every 770 persons in the department of Lima, one for every 2,500 persons in the moderately urbanized department of Arequipa, but only one for every 10,000 persons in the rest of the country.

No single set of statistics will reflect the extent to which adequate health services are available in a given country. There must be taken into account not only the supply of physicians, but the supply of other health workers, the organization of services, and the quality of these services. Similarly, it is impossible to draw up any single index to measure the progress being made in extending permanent health services in the developing countries. It is clear, however, that in most of these countries decades will be required to extend even elementary services throughout the rural areas and the fringe areas surrounding the rapidly growing cities.

ORGANIZING HEALTH SERVICES
FOR CHILDREN

The World Health Organization recommends that health services for children should be developed as an integrated part of a nation's or a community's general health services, though with a central directorate of maternal and child health to see that the special needs of children are provided for. In practice, owing to insufficient financial resources and shortages of doctors and nurses, it is sometimes more feasible to develop certain branches of health services ahead of the rest. These include mass campaigns against specific diseases that can be carried out by relatively economical chemical means of control and the extensive use of auxiliary personnel. Midwifery is frequently developed ahead of broader health services because of the possibility of using self-employed midwives to deliver babies in the home and the possibility of training traditional birth attendants to deal with normal childbirth. Furthermore, it is often feasible to develop maternal and child health (MCH) centers, particularly as sponsored and operated by voluntary organizations, as an "advance health sector." Any or all of these may be used to prepare the way for permanent health services to meet the needs of the entire population, and indeed health services for the child have proved one of the best ways of arousing the interest of a rural population in better health care and convincing them to provide buildings and tax support.

The basic step in organizing a permanent, general purpose health service in any area—or in integrating services established in advance into such a scheme—is usually to establish the fundamental institutional framework or "infra-structure." At the top of the pyramid of this infra-structure comes the central or provincial health department. Below this come the district health offices, each serving a population of 500,000 to 2,000,000 persons. The district health office should have a hospital and public health laboratory at its disposal, and should be the base for a team of medical and public health officers responsible for promoting and organizing health services for the district population. The members of this team will be concerned with hospitals, epidemic control, vaccinations, environmental sanitation, maternal and child health, and in general with the organization and supervision of the facilities and personnel available. Later, local health centers will be established as widely as possible throughout the district.

How this institutional infra-structure may be completed from the district level down can be illustrated by citing an example. India has a central health department and a health department in each of her fifteen states. The district health centers coming under the supervision of these state health departments have now been established and are being strengthened. At the next level below this, the Government is now trying to establish a primary health center, staffed by at least one doctor, one public health nurse, several midwives, and one sanitary inspector, in each rural community development block. (A community development block generally has a population of 30,000 to 60,000.)

The plan is to round out the structure by finally establishing as many village sub-centers as possible under each primary health center, each sub-center to be staffed by a midwife or auxiliary worker. The sub-centers are to be visited by the staff from the primary center once a week to hold clinics and supervise the sub-center's work. In this way, the services of one doctor may be spread over 30,000 or more people, as against the 1,000 persons typically served by a doctor in the economically advanced countries. By the end of India's Third Five Year Plan (1961-6), it is hoped to have a primary health center in each of the nation's 5,000 community development blocks so that the entire rural population will be covered, though by no means so intensively as is needed. A comparable network of urban health services is also being developed.

PROGRAMS TO EXTEND HEALTH SERVICES

Most countries have plans to extend their health services. They are generally working toward a combination of health and medical services, or, as this is sometimes phrased, preventive and curative services, and are trying to extend these into rural areas. This means the strengthening of the "infra-structure," and the gradual establishment of a network of centers which, under different names, is usually similar to the pattern of primary health centers and sub-centers described above for India. At each level, there will be special consideration for maternal and child health services. For example, the health center and sub-centers will be concerned with prenatal and postnatal checkups, delivery care, home visits, sick and well baby clinics, immunization, and education of mothers and older girls in hygiene, child rearing, and nutrition.

The most important help that can be given from the outside is for the training of personnel, and considerable bilateral aid goes for this purpose. Under the technical guidance of the World Health Organization, UNICEF makes grants at all levels of training, from the establishment of a chair of pediatrics to brief courses for traditional birth attendants.

UNICEF provides technical equipment for pediatric services in the teaching hospitals and in associated urban and rural practice areas. It may also help share the cost of the salary of a professor of pediatrics or preventive medicine for a few years in order to help establish teaching chairs in these subjects. UNICEF may also share the salaries of assistants to the professor who could thus receive training and qualify for future professorships.

To assist the upgrading and extension of rural health services, UNICEF may provide stipends so that doctors can undertake postgraduate study and so that medical officers can take refresher courses in pediatrics and preventive medicine. In some countries special efforts are being made to give some training to traditional birth attendants, commonly called "granny" midwives, so that better care during childbirth can be extended to the many women still beyond the reach of organized government health services. UNICEF has provided stipends equivalent to $7.50 to $9.00 to enable some 22,000 traditional birth attendants to receive simple additional training.

UNICEF also furnishes a variety of supplies and equipment to help extend and improve integrated health services in the developing countries. Technical equipment for public health laboratories and for obstetrical and pediatric wards in district hospitals may be provided. At the health center level, UNICEF aid may include, among other things, simple technical equipment: nurses' and midwives' kits; drugs, milk, and vitamins; a motor vehicle and bicycles to enable the center's staff to travel about in the area they serve and hold clinics in the villages. UNICEF aid has been approved for over 1,000 district centers or hospital wards, over 7,000 primary centers, and over 17,000 village sub-centers.

ENVIRONMENTAL SANITATION

It is probable that diarrheal diseases account for 30 to 50 per cent of the infant mortality in some areas, and a somewhat lower mortality but high morbidity in toddlers and children of pre-school age. Parasitic infestation, commonly associated with malnutrition and low standards of living, is also very widespread. Prevention of these conditions depends largely on health education and environmental sanitation.

The World Health Organization has stated that sufficient pure water to provide for all personal and household requirements, including sanitation, comfort, and cleanliness, is the foundation, not only of public health, but of community improvement and economic and social progress. Facilities for the sanitary disposal of excreta, and community education in the principles of personal hygiene, are other important aspects of environmental sanitation, particularly in the more densely populated areas. UNICEF can provide drilling and digging equipment for wells and latrines; piping and pumps to raise water from tube wells and bring it to village distribution points, health centers, and schools; equipment for workshops to fabricate latrine components; health education materials; and stipends to train sanitarians.

In 1959, WHO began to recommend greater emphasis on safe and ample community water supplies as a "spearhead" for promoting environmental sanitation. In line with this, UNICEF expects to increase its assistance to projects for piping greater volumes of water from nearby wells into villages and small towns to be distributed through convenient fountains and hydrants in public squares.

24

HEALTH EDUCATION

While adverse environmental conditions are an important factor in sickness among children, much ill-health is also due to ignorance of the principles of child health and nutrition, pseudo-medical beliefs, and superstition. What is needed is knowledge, and that knowledge must be imparted to the people of the less developed countries. Little can be done to improve the standards of child welfare in the home unless the parents are well enough educated to follow the advice they may be given at the health center or clinic.

Not only does health education play an essential role in the prevention of disease; it also helps overcome the resistance of individuals or groups to innovations and improvements and provides a valuable means of enlisting the active cooperation of the people in public health programs. There are excellent opportunities to instruct the women of a community when they bring their children to local centers that provide integrated preventive and curative services. The local or district hospital provides further opportunities: for example, when the mother stays with her sick child while he is in the hospital, as is the practice in many countries, she will later imitate the methods she has seen cure her child.

But broader health education measures are needed, since health centers and hospitals do not yet reach many of the people in the less developed countries. Furthermore, it is not just the mothers who must be instructed, for there are many places where, according to prevailing traditions, the young mother has little to say about how things are done in the home and where the grandmother or mother-in-law may be the person in charge of the household. To accomplish lasting results, all the women of a community must be reached—and the men, too, since their beliefs inevitably influence those of the women.

One way health education can be brought to village women is through the women's section of a community development project. For example, village women's clubs may be formed to study mothercraft and homecraft, including the basic principles of child health, nutrition, and environmental sanitation. Sometimes community health education for both men and women can be carried out through after-hours instruction at the elementary school. By first getting the parents of their pupils to attend these courses, teachers may persuade many of the adults of the community to participate. Furthermore, so that the hold of harmful traditional beliefs and practices may be broken in the future, the essentials of health and nutrition must be made a part of the basic elementary school curriculum. In short, the child at school must be given the health and nutrition education he will need to be a good parent when he has come of age.

While international assistance can play a valuable role in promoting community health education, methods of instruction and educational materials must be developed locally so that they will be suited to existing conditions and resources as found in various parts of the world. UNICEF has allocated funds for training primary school teachers in health education and for the preparation of educational materials. WHO has awarded fellowships for the training of health personnel; it has sponsored regional seminars on health education; and it has attempted to strengthen the departments of health education in various ministries of health by providing consultants and advisers.

HANDICAPPED CHILDREN AND PREMATURE INFANTS

Projects to aid physically handicapped children and save the lives of premature infants are considered relatively less urgent than other child health programs in countries which have not as yet rounded out their basic health services and where mortality rates among normal full-term infants remain high. Moreover, such projects involve relatively high costs per child benefited.

UNICEF's main contribution is to help reduce the incidence of premature births and crippling disorders through its aid to the development of basic health services and the control or eradication of certain endemic diseases. A limited amount of UNICEF aid, however, has been given to a few countries for projects dealing directly with physically handicapped children and premature infants. Emphasis has been on equipping model or pilot centers which can serve for training and demonstration purposes and which can function as a nucleus for development of a national program. UNICEF has provided modern treatment and therapy equipment for the care of physically handicapped children. For the care of premature infants, it has provided incubators and other specialized equipment.

TOTAL UNICEF AID TO PERMANENT HEALTH SERVICES

The UNICEF Executive Board voted grants totalling $7,642,000 in 1961 and $13,474,000 in 1962 to projects for the improvement of permanent health services benefiting children and mothers. UNICEF is currently assisting 156 such projects in 96 countries; 44 of these projects include special emphasis on the improvement of environmental sanitation, 9 on the rehabilitation of handicapped children, and 3 on the care of premature infants.

A NATIONAL HEALTH PROGRAM IN ACTION

Thailand provides an interesting example of how a low-income country has been able, through its own efforts, reinforced with outside aid and advice, to stretch its limited resources and build up its public health infra-structure. In 1948 a survey mission reported that there was a dire shortage of medical staff and facilities in Thailand, especially for meeting the health needs of rural children. While the national health organization extended into all the provinces, there were only 490 health centers, a mere handful of which were staffed with a doctor, to serve a rural population of some twenty million. The most important causes of illness and death among children were reported to be malaria, yaws, dysentery, and syphilis. Tuber-culosis was reported to be rampant among the juvenile population of Bangkok. An encouraging fact was that many of the existing medical per-sonnel were well trained and that many Thai doctors had received both medical and public health training in developed countries.

Beginning around 1950, the Thai Government, with considerable assist-ance from WHO and UNICEF, embarked on a systematic effort to build up its rural health services and to strengthen its training programs for all levels of medical and paramedical personnel. In a report published in 1961 the Gov-ernment was able to record "a spectacular expansion of rural health centers" and other services. Almost 800 health centers and more than 700 midwifery services centers were in operation in rural areas, and 6 MCH centers had been established in Bangkok. Two government MCH demonstration and training centers were also in operation. Special campaigns against yaws, malaria, and leprosy had been undertaken with international assistance. Yaws, the Government stated, had been practically brought under control; substantial progress had been made in malaria control; and satisfactory progress was being achieved in the campaign against leprosy. Yaws and leprosy surveillance were being integrated into the general public health organization as part of the duties of the rural health centers. A nation-wide BCG vaccination program was undertaken in 1952 to control tuberculosis, and a pilot project in more intensive methods of tuberculosis control was later conducted in Bangkok.

The number of doctors in the country increased from one per 13,600 inhabitants in 1947 to one per 7,500 inhabitants in 1960. There were also encouraging increases in the numbers of nurses, dentists, pharmacists, and midwives. But there was still a severe shortage of medical personnel in rural areas. For example, in 1957 there was one doctor for every 1,100 persons in Bangkok, but only one for every 30,000 persons in the rest of the country. The rural health centers were staffed by a total of only 90 doctors, and the services provided were "still grossly inadequate to meet the needs of the population." Indeed, the Government estimated that almost 2,400 additional doctors operating out of first-class health centers would be required to attain the desired ratio of one doctor for every 10,000 persons served through such centers. About 200 physicians a year are now being graduated from Thailand's two medical schools. A third school, which will provide 50 doctors from its first graduating class, is ready to begin its courses. The problem now is to induce a larger proportion of these new doctors and other health workers to take up rural practice. A comparable problem, it should be noted, is encountered in almost all parts of the developing world.

From 1950 through 1962 UNICEF allocated about $1,694,000 to Thailand for the development of permanent health services for children and mothers. Matching expenditures on the part of the Thai Government have come to about twice this amount. WHO has provided considerable technical support for the training of nurses and midwives and has sent promising students abroad on fellowships. WHO consultants have played an important role in helping the government assess the country's health problems and strengthen its services. Both WHO and UNICEF have assisted in the mass disease control campaigns undertaken by the Thai Government; UNICEF allocations to Thailand for mass disease control came to over $2 million for the period 1950-62. Thailand has also received important bilateral assistance in its health program. For example, the United States Government has been assisting in getting a village sanitation program under way. Representatives of UNICEF, WHO, and the United States Agency for International Development attend meetings of the Ministry of Health's coordinating committee to insure that there is no duplication of effort.

Efforts are now being made to staff health centers more adequately and establish a supervisory system covering the work of the rural midwives. Midwives are receiving courses of additional training with emphasis on public health, and short courses are being given to the traditional birth attendants (mohtamyaes), who are still the only persons available to attend the great majority of women in childbirth. Worth mentioning, as an intering example of one of the many small things that may be done to improve health services in a developing country, is the UNICEF-assisted program to teach rural nurse supervisors how to drive. This will make it possible to dispense with hired drivers. Entrusting nurses with something as valuable as a vehicle will enhance their prestige.

Campaigns against Communicable Diseases

Aside from nutritional disorders, communicable diseases are the predominant cause of sickness and death among the world's children. Some of these—infective diarrheas, the various diseases caused by intestinal parasites, common respiratory infections like bronchitis and pneumonia, such "childhood" diseases as measles and whooping cough—are not amenable to the kind of mass control techniques feasible in the less developed countries. One of the reasons for expanding basic health services as quickly as possible is to deal with these diseases.

There are, however, major communicable diseases that can be controlled, or even eradicated, through special campaigns based on some of the newer drugs, antibiotics, vaccines, and other biological or chemical weapons that have entered the public health arsenal. In campaigns against these diseases it is sometimes feasible to use a large number of local people trained specifically to carry out routine tasks under the direction of a small group of skilled technicians. Globally speaking, the diseases amenable to such "mass control" techniques that have the greatest impact on the health of children are malaria, trachoma, bilharziasis, yaws, tuberculosis, and leprosy. All of these diseases, with the exception of tuberculosis, have largely disappeared in the technologically advanced countries. Persons living in Europe, North America, and Oceania will require some imagination to conceive of them as a world problem. Yet, in many countries, one or more of these diseases place such a burden on normal health services and play such havoc with development efforts that their control must be given a high priority. Furthermore, health services directed only to children and mothers will not suffice to bring them under control, for the reservoir of infection extends to the population at large.

Extensive mass campaigns against some of these diseases have been carried out in many parts of the world in recent years. As of 1962, UNICEF had assisted 116 countries and territories in disease control campaigns, and annual UNICEF allocations for major disease control averaged $9.3 million over the period 1961-2. More children have directly benefited from these projects than from any other UNICEF-assisted activities. Some of the results have been little short of spectacular. Many of these campaigns provide outstanding examples of how drugs and chemicals originally developed in the industrially advanced countries can be effectively used in other parts of the world. Many of them also demonstrate the outstanding success that the low-income countries can achieve in developing their limited organizational and financial resources to obtain wide benefits from modern scientific discoveries. For this reason, the principal mass disease control campaigns that are being carried out with UNICEF and WHO assistance are described at some length in the remainder of this section.

MALARIA

About 35 per cent of the world's population live in areas almost entirely confined to the tropics and subtropics, where malaria is still prevalent. Another 25 per cent of the world's population live in areas* concerning which the WHO has no up-to-date information but where malaria was very prevalent in the recent past. Thus at least 1,000 million and possibly as many as 1,800 million persons are still threatened by this disease despite the very substantial efforts since World War II to bring it under control. As recently as 1955, according to WHO estimates, 200 million persons annually contracted malaria and two million died of its effects. By 1961 it was estimated that this death toll had been halved. A high proportion of deaths from malaria occur among children under fifteen, and in areas where the incidence of malaria is high, it is one of the main causes of infant and child mortality.

Malaria takes a high toll, not only in terms of human life, but in terms of human energy. In countries where it is most prevalent it seriously handicaps all efforts that directly or indirectly would serve to improve the condition of children. The child with malaria will not get the full benefit of improved schooling. Chronic malaria stunts physical and mental development, hampers the exploitation of natural resources, reduces agricultural production, and impairs industry and commerce. In short, the social and economic repercussions of malaria make it the world's most expensive disease.

Shortly before the turn of this century it was discovered that malaria is caused by miscroscopic parasites that destroy red blood cells, and that these parasites are transmitted by the bite of the female anopheles mosquito. When the mosquito bites an infected person, she sucks up a load of parasites along with the person's blood. After a 9- to 15-day incubation period, the parasites can be transmitted to a healthy person bitten by the same mosquito. The cycle of transmission can be broken if the infected mosquito is killed before the parasites incubate.

Until World War II, the best method that could be devised for malaria control was an attack on the breeding places of the vector species of anopheles mosquito, supplemented by the use of quinine and other anti-malarial drugs. Since mosquitoes can breed in the amount of water that collects in a hollow tree or a tin can, it was impossible to make much headway in rural

---

* Mainland China, North Korea, North Viet-Nam.

areas. A major breakthrough came soon after the War with the discovery that the transmission cycle of the malaria parasite can be broken by spraying the inside walls of dwellings with DDT or other long-lasting insecticides.

The anopheles is a nocturnal mosquito. After feeding off her victim, she is heavy and generally rests on the wall of the room. If the wall has been sprayed with an insecticide, the mosquito will die before the incubation period of the parasite is completed and before she can transmit the infection to another person. With this discovery, not only malaria control, but malaria eradication became feasible. For, unless they are reintroduced, malaria parasites usually disappear from the blood of their human hosts within three years. Hence, if a break in the man-mosquito-man cycle can be continuously maintained through systematic spraying for three years or more, malaria can be eradicated even though all the vector species will usually not have been eradicated.

A malaria campaign generally begins with a preparatory phase, requiring at least a year, during which the malarious areas are surveyed, detailed plans made, and personnel trained. Then follows the attack phase, lasting three, four, or more years, during which the inside of every habitation must be sprayed with insecticide, usually twice a year. Then in the consolidation phase, the remaining reservoirs of human infection are located by case-finding, and dealt with by spraying and anti-malarial drugs. After at least three years of such surveillance, the regular permanent health services, suitably strengthened, can be relied on to protect the population against any reintroduction of the disease.

The government representatives who assembled in Mexico City for the Eighth World Health Assembly in 1955 agreed that the time had come for a world-wide effort to stamp out malaria, and in the same year the UNICEF Executive Board decided to join with WHO and the United States International Cooperation Administration (now AID) in a large-scale operation to help countries carry out complete eradication programs by as early a date as possible.

By 1962 WHO was able to report very impressive results along the world-wide front. Eradication programs were in progress in areas with a total population of 748 million in Asia, the Eastern Mediterranean, and Latin America. Zanzibar has the only eradication program in tropical Africa; pre-eradication programs are being planned in other countries. Eradication programs had reached the consolidation phase in large areas of Mexico, Turkey, Jordan, India, Iraq, Iran, and Syria. Eradication had been successfully completed in southern Europe, southern United States, Singapore, Puerto Rico, northern Venezuela, and a few small areas elsewhere in the tropics. Eradication campaigns have not yet been undertaken in all malarious regions. International agencies do not encourage governments to undertake

31

eradication programs until their administrative and health services have reached a certain level. In most of tropical Africa, international aid is being directed to these necessary "pre-eradication" developments.

A considerable financial effort has been called for to launch the world fight against malaria. Total eradication expenditures for the period 1958-60 averaged $94 million a year, coming from the following sources:

Countries with malaria	$53.3 million
United States bilateral aid	22.5 million
UNICEF	9.0 million
WHO	5.5 million
Pan American Health Organization	2.7 million
United Nations Technical Assistance	0.7 million
	$93.7 million

It has been estimated that between $1 and $2 billion will be necessary to complete the job of eradication in the countries for which information is available.

UNICEF aid to malaria eradication takes the form of insecticides, sprayers, vehicles, anti-malarial drugs, and in some cases laboratory equipment and supplies. In 1962, insecticides provided by UNICEF were being used to combat malaria in 34 different countries and were protecting some 46 million persons, about half of them children and mothers. In recent years UNICEF's contribution to the malaria campaign has been the largest single item among its allocations, accounting for over one-third. In 1961 the Executive Board decided that, in view of the great importance of malaria eradication to the health and welfare of children, support should be continued at least to January, 1964, when it would review the question. However, in order to allow UNICEF to increase its aid to governments in dealing with other problems they might find to be among the most critical affecting their children, the Board decided that its allocations for the fight against malaria should not exceed $10 million a year.

One of the best examples of an eradication program is Mexico's, now nearing completion. The cost has been high, and extensive operations have been necessary. To cover expenditures from the beginning of the campaign in 1955 through the year 1961, the Mexican Government had appropriated more than $25 million; UNICEF had allocated about $10 million, and WHO/PAHO about $1 million, including some United Nations Technical Assistance funds. By jeep, on horseback, by motorboat, and on foot, some 2,800 men, each carrying with him 15 kilograms of spraying equipment, have crisscrossed the country time and again. During the first half of 1960 alone more than three million houses were sprayed.

To carry the program through to the end of 1964, by which time it is expected that the consolidation phase will be completed, another $11 million will be required. Thus the total cost of the campaign will come to at least $47 million. This figure hardly compares, however, with the cost that malaria itself exacted when the campaign began. At that time it was estimated that malaria affected two million persons every year and that the annual economic loss to the country came to more than $160 million. How well the campaign has succeeded can be suggested by the fact that during 1960 not a single death was confirmed as attributable to malaria. At the 1961 meeting of the UNICEF Executive Board the representatives of Mexico announced that the government was drawing up plans to move several million persons from the overcrowded central plateau and resettle them in formerly malarious lands along the coast.

YAWS AND RELATED DISEASES

Yaws, a communicable disease usually acquired in childhood, is caused by an organism closely related to that which causes syphilis. Both yaws and syphilis are grouped in a family of diseases called the treponematoses. Warmth and humidity favor the transmission of yaws, and in rural areas of the tropics where primitive living conditions, crowded quarters, and poor sanitation prevail, contagion spreads quickly. Starting with a small raspberry-like sore (whence the medical name "frambosia"), the disease, if untreated, takes on many different patterns. Ulcerous sores often appear on the soles of the feet, so that the victim cannot walk, or on the palms of the hands, so that he cannot work. The disease eats away soft body tissues and may attack the bones. Sufferers seldom die from yaws, but they are frequently disfigured and may be crippled for life.

Around 1946 the incidence of yaws and syphilis was at its post-war peak in most parts of the world. It was estimated at the time that there were some 50 million cases of yaws, 20 million cases of venereal syphilis, and possibly a million cases of endemic non-venereal syphilis.

In the post-war period, as long-acting penicillin preparations became increasingly available, many countries organized programs aimed at eradicating these diseases, for penicillin has proved a veritable miracle drug in the treatment of the treponematoses: yaws, for example, can usually be cured in 15 days with one injection of long-acting penicillin and at an average cost, examination and treatment included, of about 70 cents.

A campaign against yaws begins with a preliminary survey to determine its actual prevalence. This is followed by community-wide examination and treatment, either by house-to-house visiting or by assembling groups of people in convenient places. Examination of less than 90 per cent of the population is considered inadequate, and 100 per cent coverage is the goal.

The aim of the campaign is, not just to cure all active cases, but to remove the reservoir of community infection by treating contacts and latent cases as well as all active cases.

Resurveys are conducted from time to time until it is found that the incidence has fallen to a level that can be handled by normal health services. Auxiliaries used in the mass campaigns against yaws may then be trained for broader health activities. To achieve complete yaws eradication, initial successes must be consolidated and anti-yaws work integrated into strengthened local rural health services, which popular interest aroused by a successful campaign can help to create.

The greatest reservoirs of yaws have been found in West Africa and Southeast Asia. With the aid of UNICEF and WHO, nearly all the countries with a high incidence of this disease have now started campaigns which, if extended over a number of years until all affected areas have been covered, should reduce it to a minor public health problem. UNICEF aid takes the form of penicillin, syringes, blood-test supplies, and transport. UNICEF has aided, in all, 52 countries and territories to combat yaws and related diseases. In 1962 it was assisting 20 yaws control projects and 4 syphilis control projects. By 1962, in UNICEF-assisted programs, more than 85 million persons had been examined for yaws and more than 34 million had been treated; more than 7 million had been examined for syphilis and about 3.3 million had been treated. UNICEF allocations for the control of these diseases have been averaging about $200,000 annually.

About a third of the job of combating yaws throughout the world had been accomplished by 1962. Asia was the continent where the widest results had been achieved: while some 30 million persons, mostly in Indonesia, where the campaign has only recently been extended beyond the island of Java, were still exposed to the disease, yaws had been effectively brought under control in areas with a population of about 50 million, and mass campaigns were in progress in other parts of the continent with a population of about 30 million. In Africa, the principal remaining reservoir of infection, anti-yaws campaigns were under way in 14 different countries.

A successful yaws campaign demonstrates dramatically the efficacy of modern disease control techniques and provides an excellent opportunity to mobilize popular support for more extensive rural health measures. The yaws campaign that was carried out with UNICEF assistance in the Nsukka area of eastern Nigeria is a case in point. When the campaign was begun, early in 1954, 10 to 15 per cent of the population were found to have yaws in an infectious or late stage. Hence universal mass treatment was decided on. Simple dispensaries were set up throughout the area, and the cooperation of the village headmen was enlisted. More than 96 per cent of the people in the area turned out for the first round of examinations and treatments. Village youths were trained as "yaws scouts" to locate new and recurring cases and bring them in for treatment. Within six months the number of infectious cases had been cut to one-thirtieth their previous level. A secondary benefit was the virtual disappearance of gonorrhea, previously very prevalent.

Before the Nsukka yaws campaign was inaugurated, plans for a network of coordinated rural health centers in the area had been held up for lack of local funds. With the success of the yaws campaign before their eyes, the locally-elected district councillors quickly approved the necessary support for the health centers. By the end of 1955, seven of these centers had been opened, and the "yaws scouts" had been given further training so that they could act as health visitors. So successful has the Nsukka rural health scheme proved that it is now serving as a demonstration and training area for all of eastern Nigeria.

TRACHOMA AND RELATED EYE INFECTIONS

Trachoma, a painful eye infection that damages the eyelids and cornea, affects an estimated 400 million persons and is regarded as the greatest single cause of partial or complete blindness in the world today. It is especially prevalent in the dry, sandy areas of Africa, the Eastern Mediterranean, Pakistan, north India, and parts of east Asia. Described as "a disease of poverty and overcrowding," trachoma appears to be most frequently transmitted through close family contact and is almost always contracted in infancy. If untreated, it becomes a chronic condition remaining with the victim throughout his life. Though itself a virus disease, trachoma is often complicated by bacterial infections. For example, in North Africa and the Middle East, it is frequently aggravated by acute conjunctivitis, a bacterial disease that regularly occurs as a seasonal epidemic, affecting 80 to 100 per cent of the population in many communities.

Effective and economical methods for control of trachoma are still under study. By the early 1950's it had been found that certain of the broad-spectrum antibiotics were effective against the disease. Trials conducted in Morocco against trachoma and associated conjunctivitis gave encouraging indications that a relatively economical method of collective treatment might work. Twice daily for three consecutive days a 1 per cent ointment of the antibiotic chlor-tetra-cycline was applied to the eyes of children with trachoma. This cycle of treatment was repeated every four weeks for a period of 20 weeks. Enough cases were cleared up to lead to its being widely used in Morocco. Later on, to reduce the drain on public health services, the Moroccan Government began to teach people to apply the ointment themselves when follow-up treatments are called for.

Though the schedule of treatments worked out in Morocco has not proved satisfactory everywhere, collective treatment with local applications of antibiotics is now the standard procedure in mass campaigns against trachoma. While hundreds of thousands of cases have been cured, new cases continue to appear. With the present drugs it is necessary to continue treatment campaigns indefinitely—until living conditions and health education are considerably improved. The search for more effective anti-trachoma drugs is continuing. The trachoma virus has been isolated, and the possibilities of developing immunization measures against trachoma are being explored.

UNICEF can provide antibiotics, laboratory and diagnostic equipment, health education materials, and transport for campaigns against trachoma and related eye diseases. In 1962 UNICEF and WHO were assisting 16 countries in such campaigns—9 in North Africa and the Near East, 5 in Asia, and 2 in southern Europe. Several other countries have been receiving drugs for the treatment of eye diseases through their regular MCH centers.

By 1962 almost ten million children had been treated in UNICEF-assisted projects, and it was expected that 2 million more would be treated in the course of the year. UNICEF allocated $1,069,000 for the control of trachoma and related infections in 1962.

The largest school treatment program to date has been carried out in Taiwan. By 1956 all Taiwanese school children had been examined for trachoma, and more than a million had been treated. A home treatment program began in 1958. The Government has now launched a six-year program aimed at complete control of trachoma throughout the island. In households where there are two or more cases of trachoma, all members of the household will be treated. In areas where the disease is most prevalent, entire communities will be treated.

Globally speaking, it should be emphasized, these campaigns have reached no more than a handful out of every hundred children suffering from trachoma. In the countries where intensive campaigns have not been extended beyond the schools, the large reservoirs of infection among younger children and children who do not attend school have hardly been touched. But the aid WHO and UNICEF are providing to help governments improve their basic public health services and raise levels of environmental sanitation will, in the long run, also help to reduce the incidence of trachoma in many parts of the world.

LEPROSY

Leprosy, in certain of its forms one of the most hideously disfiguring diseases known to man, was, until very recently, surrounded by an aura of mystery and horror. In Medieval Europe lepers were regarded as legally dead; when a person was pronounced a leper, he was given the last rites of the Church and banished from the community. The belief that leprosy is incurable and that lepers are an accursed minority, specially singled out for supernatural punishment, persists in many areas and is a serious obstacle that must be overcome before people can be persuaded to treat leprosy victims as they would treat the victims of any other serious disease.

It has now been proved that leprosy is not a highly contagious disease —it is not so contagious as tuberculosis, for example—and it has been proved that leprosy can be cured. Persons with open lesions constitute the greatest source of contagion; but they represent a small proportion of total cases. The closed forms are practically all non-contagious. Beginning in 1943, methods of treatment were developed with some of the sulfone drugs that can quickly arrest the progress of the disease and reduce the infectiousness of active cases. All cases that are caught when the first signs of the disease appear can now easily be cured. The most useful of the anti-leprosy drugs is diamino-diphenyl-sulfone, or DDS. Leprosy control projects assisted by UNICEF and WHO have confirmed the effectiveness of mass treatment based on DDS and the feasibility of organizing mass detection and treatment services even in remote rural areas.

Susceptibility to leprosy is greatest in childhood. The child who contracts leprosy may become a permanent invalid by the time he comes of age. About a quarter of all leprosy patients, it is estimated, suffer some kind of permanent physical disability as a result of the disease.

In 1959 WHO reported that at least two million cases of leprosy were registered with the appropriate authorities throughout the world, and that three-quarters of these were under treatment. The actual number of cases was estimated by some authorities at 10 to 12 million. The number of registered cases has been rising in recent years, but this is a sign of progress rather than a cause for alarm, for it means that an increasing number of sufferers are no longer ashamed or afraid to report for examination and treatment. Africa and Asia are considered the world's most important reservoirs of leprosy —Chad, Ghana, Nigeria, and Senegal; Burma, India, and Thailand being some of the countries most seriously affected. Though not so prevalent in any part of the Americas as in Africa, leprosy is a problem in Brazil, Colombia, and Venezuela. The disease is endemic in many of the islands of the Southwest Pacific.

Leprosy has largely disappeared in those parts of the world where higher standards of living prevail. Any measures which raise general levels of public health, whether directed against specific infections or aimed at improving nutrition, sanitation, or housing, are likely to help in the control of leprosy. Ideally, leprosy control should be integrated into general health work from the start. Since the disease is often most prevalent in remote rural areas, however, this approach is not generally feasible. Fortunately, a good beginning can often be achieved through special leprosy campaigns initiated before it is possible to place health centers throughout the area.

The first phase is one of mass case finding and treatment. Case finding can sometimes be combined with another mass disease control campaign, one against yaws, for example. DDS is comparatively easy to administer orally or through injections. However, if treatment is to be effective it must be carried out regularly for years, during which time the drug must be administered twice a week if taken orally or twice a month if given through injections. "Case-holding" is thus the most critical aspect of leprosy treatment.

Since the infectiousness of "open" cases of leprosy can now be reduced very quickly, it is no longer considered necessary or desirable to segregate all lepers in special colonies or "leprosaria" as was once done. Patients generally continue to live at home, and go regularly to a neighboring treatment point. Each leprosy worker, usually travelling by bicycle, serves a circuit of such treatment points. (In some of the more sparsely settled parts of Africa where this is impractical, persons suffering from leprosy are brought together in special villages for the early stages of treatment. They are encouraged to return home once the disease has reached the non-infectious stage.) Institutions are now used chiefly for the treatment of disabled cases or others so seriously ill that they require special care.

Modern leprosy control strategy provides an excellent example of "prevention through mass treatment." While the cure of persons suffering from the early stages of leprosy and the rehabilitation of those suffering from the later stages of the disease are important humanitarian considerations, the primary objective of mass campaigns is to protect future generations, for this is what will be accomplished if all present victims—children and adults alike—can be found and treated.

UNICEF began aiding leprosy control campaigns in 1953 and by 1962 had provided sulfone drugs and other supplies and equipment to help carry out projects in 35 countries—20 in Africa, 7 in Asia, 5 in the Americas, 2 in the Eastern Mediterranean, and 1 (Solomon Islands) in the Pacific. All except the Solomon Islands project were still receiving assistance in 1962, and more than a million persons, half of them mothers and children, were being treated through these projects. This represents about one-tenth of the world total of cases. Annual allocations for leprosy control average about $800,000.

TUBERCULOSIS

Tuberculosis, a disease that spares no ethnic group or social system, is a world-wide health problem: it is highly prevalent among the Eskimos of the Arctic as well as among the peoples of the tropics. At the beginning of the

19th century, the growing industrial cities of Europe and North America had tuberculosis mortality rates of 400 or more per 100,000 inhabitants per year. By 1900 this mortality rate had fallen to about 200 in the United States, and its drop over the next 60 years was dramatic; by 1960 it had fallen to the very low level of 6 per 100,000. Comparable declines occurred in western Europe, Australia, and other economically advanced areas.

Today there are still many parts of the world where tuberculosis death rates in excess of 100 per 100,000 inhabitants persist. It is feared that tuberculosis will be a particularly serious problem in the rapidly growing urban slums of the tropics and subtropics, where poor living conditions, a shortage of protein in the diet, and overcrowding favor the spread of the disease and aggravate its effects.

Though the clinical manifestations of tuberculosis of the lungs usually first appear in adolescence or early adulthood, the infection is very often acquired in childhood. The earlier preventive measures can be taken, the better. Tests indicate that in many less developed countries more than 40 per cent of the children have acquired tuberculosis infections by the age of fourteen. While perhaps only a small percentage of these will develop active tuberculosis, all are seriously threatened by the disease. Tuberculosis, it should be noted, attacks other organs as well as the lungs. If acquired in infancy, the infection is likely to become widely disseminated throughout the body with fatal results. Tubercular meningitis—a disease of the membranes enveloping the brain and spinal cord—accounted for 44 per cent of the deaths among children who were admitted to one of the larger hospitals in New Delhi in the period 1955-8.

In the United States it costs, on the average, about $20,000 to find and treat a case of active tuberculosis through classic methods involving mass X-ray examination and the prolonged hospitalization of the more serious cases. Such a costly approach is plainly out of the question for the less developed countries. Fortunately, in many of these countries, it does appear feasible to attack tuberculosis with specialized weapons provided by modern science: BCG vaccination, and the new anti-tuberculosis drugs, principally isoniazid.

BCG vaccine consists of living cultures of bovine tubercle bacilli whose virulence has been reduced by growing them in a special medium over many years. (BCG stands for *Bacillus Calmette-Guérin,* Calmette and Guérin being the two French scientists who cultured the first strain and produced the first vaccine.) BCG provides about 75 to 80 per cent protection against clinical tuberculosis to persons not already infected by virulent tubercle bacilli who are exposed to a significant risk of infection.

For persons who are already infected, the new drugs are the principal hope to have appeared in the past ten years. Home treatment appears to be almost as effective as treatment in a hospital—provided that treatment is prolonged, uninterrupted, and that the drugs are administered in adequate doses and in the prescribed manner. This is a very important proviso, however, and it would be foolish to expect too much from home therapy in most of the less developed countries until popular health education has greatly progressed, until thousands of doctors, nurses and health visitors have been trained, and until appropriate services have been organized.

National and international efforts to combat tuberculosis in the less developed countries have, accordingly, been concentrated on two immediate measures that between them promise to bring tuberculosis control into sight as an attainable objective:

- BCG vaccination of all children and other vulnerable groups whom tuberculin tests show to be free of infection.

- Establishing the framework for a program of case finding and ambulatory treatment in areas where the prevalence of active tuberculosis is highest.

The technique employed in mass tuberculin testing and BCG vaccination by mobile teams using a substantial proportion of auxiliary personnel were developed in the Scandinavian countries, and from 1948 to 1951 UNICEF aid to countries for testing and vaccination campaigns was carried out jointly with Scandinavian welfare organizations. Beginning in 1951 UNICEF and WHO became partners in this program. By 1962, UNICEF had aided 65 countries with BCG campaigns, in which 346 million children and young adults had been tested and 134 million vaccinated. Thirteen campaigns were still in progress.

By 1960 it appeared that, outside of tropical Africa, most of the countries requiring international assistance to launch mass testing and BCG campaigns had taken advantage of UNICEF/WHO aid to do so. Emphasis is now shifting to the necessary continuing activity: vaccination of children born since the original campaigns were carried out and periodic re-vaccination of the others. The goal is to have this carried on by the regular health centers as soon as enough can be opened. Since the cumulative chances of infection increase with every year of childhood, children should be protected as soon in life as possible. In mass campaigns greater effort is being made to vaccinate toddlers and pre-school children, even though they are harder to reach than school children.

As BCG vaccination confers no benefit on persons who have ever been infected—and these may include a high proportion of the apparently healthy young people in a given community—BCG campaigns should, as soon as this is feasible, be combined with other public health measures to combat tuberculosis. By 1962 UNICEF was assisting 35 countries to take the first steps necessary to establish permanent anti-tuberculosis services. An increasing amount of UNICEF aid has been going to national pilot-area projects designed to find the best means of adapting control measures to local conditions and to train a nucleus of national personnel. In all, UNICEF is now allocating over $1 million a year to BCG campaigns and tuberculosis control projects. The main items furnished are vehicles for mass campaigns, diagnostic X-ray apparatus, and drugs.

The largest scale attempt to deal with tuberculosis on a national level is being undertaken by the Government of India. A tuberculin testing and BCG vaccination program was inaugurated in 1951 with UNICEF and WHO assistance. In 1956 the Government decided to integrate this into an intensive, long-term control program. To establish the framework for this larger program, a national tuberculosis institute, a control and training center in each of the 16 states, 380 district centers, and a number of mobile diagnostic units are envisaged. Under the Second Five-Year Plan (1956-61) the equivalent of more than $13 million was earmarked by India for these projects. During this period UNICEF allocated about $1.3 million to the Indian Government for laboratory and X-ray equipment, aid to train the necessary personnel, and transport. By the end of 1961, the national institute, about half the proposed state centers, and a number of the district centers were in operation. At this point in the program's development, pilot areas covering rural and urban populations of 20 million had been brought under coverage. The ultimate goal will be to extend control methods worked out in these pilot areas to the nation.

BILHARZIASIS

Bilharziasis is a parasitic disease second in its world impact only to malaria. Several related species of small fresh water snails serve in different regions as intermediate host for the parasite, and the disease is sometimes called "snail fever." The life cycle of the *Schistosoma* fluke, the tiny parasitic worm that causes bilharziasis, is a complex one. The adult worms live in the blood vessels of their human victims. Their eggs are excreted in human urine or feces. When these reach fresh water, they hatch. The larvae that emerge from these eggs must find suitable snail hosts within a certain time or perish. After the parasites have multiplied for several generations within these snails, free swimming larvae of a different kind are released. These bore through the skin or mucous membranes of persons wading, bathing in, or drinking the infested water. The larvae make their way to the liver, mature, and mate. The cycle then begins over again.

Bilharziasis is usually acquired in middle or late childhood, but the disease may last for the better part of the victim's lifetime even if he is not rein-

41

fected, for the adult flukes can survive 20 to 30 years in the bloodstream. In areas where the disease is prevalent, a very high proportion of children are likely to become infected by the age of twelve, showing blood in their urine and a variety of other symptoms. The disease damages various organs and, though not fatal in most cases, saps the victim's energy and retards his mental development. Ironically enough, in many parts of the world the vast irrigation systems constructed to improve the standard of living have had the effect of undermining the people's health, for the networks of canals have proved ideally suited for the propagation of the species of snails that spread bilharziasis. (As a matter of fact, the disease can be traced back to the dawn of large-scale irrigation: eggs of the *Schistosoma* parasite have been found in the kidneys of Egyptian mummies dating from 1250-1000 B.C.) WHO estimated in the late 1950's that 150 million persons suffered from the disease, including at least 33 million in China, 12 million in Egypt, 7 million in west and central Africa, and 4 million in Brazil.

No really satisfactory method of bilharziasis control has yet been found. Good environmental sanitation is effective in breaking the cycle of transmission, and is the proper long-term solution. Because of the slow process of health education of the public, and the cost of providing pure water supplies, supplementary measures are being sought that will hasten the results. Certain anti-bilharziasis drugs exist, but none is suitable for mass treatment. Attacking the snails that act as intermediate hosts for the parasite seems to be the most promising approach, and there are effective molluscicides— substances which, added to the water in very minute amounts will kill the snails without harming human beings or other animals. The problem is to apply these to continuously moving and continuously re-infected waters.

Bilharziasis is one of the few diseases affecting large numbers of children that actually appears to be on the increase today. To further the development of effective methods of combatting this disease, the UNICEF Executive Board in March 1959 decided to aid pilot projects for bilharziasis control. Two of these had got under way by 1961—one in Egypt, where the incidence of infection was reported to be 42 per cent, and one on Leyte, where in some areas almost half the population suffered from the disease, children ten to fourteen years of age being the most severely affected.

UNICEF POLICY OF ASSISTANCE
TO DISEASE CONTROL CAMPAIGNS

UNICEF has helped governments undertake campaigns against one or more of the above diseases when the following conditions prevail:

1. The disease is a predominant cause of sickness among children or a major disease usually acquired and best prevented in childhood.

2. Known measures of prevention or control can be effectively carried out at a low cost per person under existing field conditions. This implies that a large part of the necessary work can be carried out by non-professional auxiliaries.

3. It seems likely that the gains won in the campaign can eventually be held by the regular national health services.

The goal is to reduce and, if possible, wipe out the reservoir of infection over large areas and by so doing to protect the children of future generations. For this reason, UNICEF aid is granted only to campaigns against individual diseases when aimed at complete coverage of a given area or population group, or to pilot projects that may lead to such campaigns. A disease control campaign, to be eligible for UNICEF assistance, must not merely be directed to the cure of individual cases, but must have important preventive and public health aspects.

CHAPTER III
Food and Nutrition

Hunger is one of the most important factors contributing to the sufferings of children and to the waste of human resources in vast areas of the world today. B. R. Sen, the Director-General of FAO, recently estimated that from one-third to one-half of the world's population suffer from undernourishment or malnutrition. This includes between 300 million and 500 million persons who, even in normal times, do not get enough food of any description, and as many as a billion more who do not receive an adequately balanced diet. Persons concerned with the welfare of children find themselves inescapably involved in problems of nutrition, for in areas where inadequate family diets prevail, children are the first to suffer. It is likely that well over half the world's children suffer from serious dietary deficiencies at some time during their early childhood.

The cost of hunger is a high one, and it is only within the past twenty years that it has begun to be fully appreciated. Malnutrition, unlike most of the communicable diseases, is often a slow, insidious process. Its manifestations are frequently masked by the more dramatic symptoms of other disorders, to which it contributes by undermining the body's resistance. While a close relation between diet and health has been postulated since the days of Hippocrates, even the medical profession, until very recently, was not fully aware of the serious disorders caused by certain common nutritional deficiencies, particularly among children.

It is only recently, too, that the extent to which undernourishment and malnutrition may impede a people's economic and social development has been appreciated. Chronic hunger has turned out to be less of a spur, as it was long regarded, than a crippling impediment, for the fact is that poorly fed people do not have the physical or mental energy to solve their own problems. Improvements in the diet of workers have often been followed by sharp increases in their productivity; in many instances the classroom achievement of school children has also sharply improved when they have been provided with supplementary meals.

The damage inflicted by undernourishment and malnutrition may begin early in life. Pre-school children hospitalized for severe protein malnutrition are frequently so dull and apathetic that they will remain sitting wherever they are placed until they are lifted up again. They never, as do so many other children, go wandering off to investigate matters for themselves. These alterations in the child's personality may persist even if he recovers physically. If this happens widely enough, apathy can become one of the cultural characteristics of the general population of an area. Thus, not only the individual child, but the country as a whole is the loser.

THE NATURAL HISTORY OF
MALNUTRITION IN CHILDREN

Two general factors appear to be largely responsible for the fact that the majority of the world's children fare as poorly as they do: the inadequate development of agriculture in most of the technologically underdeveloped world and the widespread ignorance of the special nutritional needs of children. The results follow logically enough. In some of the less developed countries there is simply not enough food of any description to go around. In many more there is not enough of the right kind of food to go around. And even when the right foods could be found locally, parents often do not realize the need to give these foods to their children.

The simple lack of enough food to cover a person's energy requirements, as measured in calories, is usually described as "undernourishment." Carbohydrates—starches and sugars—provide most of the world's food energy. In the developing countries the reliance on carbohydrates is particularly marked. But, in addition to sufficient calories, an adequate diet must provide minimum amounts of at least 43 specific chemical substances identified as amino acids (the constituents of proteins), vitamins, mineral elements, and certain fatty acids. These are substances the body needs but cannot synthesize on its own, and a shortage of any of them over a long enough period will induce specific starvation symptoms. Such deficiencies are usually described as "malnutrition."

Children are hardest hit by nutritional deficiencies during their years of most rapid growth, which may be described as extending from the moment of conception through gestation, infancy, and up to about the age of four. For every kilogram of body weight, the six month old infant needs about twice as many calories and about five times as much high-quality protein as the average adult; the two year old, about 70 per cent more calories and about three times as much high-quality protein as the average adult; the four year old, about 50 per cent more calories and about twice as much protein as the average adult. Thus, the child needs not only more food, in proportion to his weight, than the adult; he needs food of a considerably higher quality.

46

Care for the child's nutrition begins logically with improvement of the mother's nutrition during pregnancy and lactation. Poor maternal nutrition is thought to be responsible for many miscarriages, stillbirths, and premature births. However, the old adage that, if necessary, the child in the womb takes what he needs at the mother's expense would seem to carry some force; for, on the average, in poorly fed areas full term infants weigh only 250 to 500 grams less than those born in Europe or North America. The great majority of these children, too, are successfully nursed by their mothers. Unfortunately, in many urban areas of the tropics there is a growing tendency to introduce bottle feeding at an early age, probably in mistaken emulation of European and North American mores of a decade or more ago. If standards of home sanitation are poor and if adequate substitutes for breast milk are hard to come by—and such is usually the case—early bottle feeding is extremely dangerous.

The child who is successfully breast fed will generally be adequately nourished until at least the age of six months. This is shown by the fact that the height and weight curves of babies in the less developed areas usually parallel the growth curves of babies in the economically developed countries up to that age. From then on, however, the right foods are generally not introduced to supplement breast milk. In rural areas, nursing is frequently prolonged for a year or two. Extended nursing will usually protect the child from the more dramatic symptoms of malnutrition, even though his growth will be retarded if adequate supplements are not forthcoming. It is when the child is completely weaned, some time between the age of one and three years, that the most dangerous period begins.

The child of the tropics and subtropics who has just been weaned will generally have to survive on a diet high in starches but low in proteins, vitamins, and certain essential mineral elements. Where custom prescribes special foods for children of this age, these are generally bland, starchy preparations—based on bananas, cassava (manioc), arrowroot, maize, rice gruel, and the like—and they are often even less nutritious than the foods the rest of the family eats. If the child gets sick, "rich foods" are frequently blamed and his diet is likely to be still further restricted to starchy gruels. Serious malnutrition can itself impair the child's ability to digest certain foods—whole milk, for example—and the vicious circle so formed can lead to death unless proper treatment is forthcoming.

Children who survive to school age are in a much better position to adapt to the adult household diet, inadequate though this may be; but in the poorest areas of the world they, too, often suffer from undernourishment and malnutrition. The ability of children of this age to learn and to keep up with their school work has often improved dramatically when special supplementary meals have been provided for them.

PRINCIPAL NUTRITIONAL DISORDERS OF CHILDREN
IN THE TROPICS AND SUBTROPICS

A pediatrician in one of the economically advanced countries might pass his entire career without examining a single child suffering from some of the forms of malnutrition that are commonest in the tropics and subtropics. Some of these—protein malnutrition and acute vitamin A deficiency, for example—have never, so far as is known, been grave problems in most of the temperate regions, with the possible exception of China and Japan. Others—endemic goitre and rickets, for example—have been practically eliminated in the economically advanced countries within the past forty years. On the other hand, some of the forms of malnutrition to which this pediatrician would be most alert—vitamin C deficiency, for example—are rare in the tropics and subtropics, owing to the abundance of fresh fruits.

Undernutrition, a polite word for semi-starvation, is still a much more common cause of sickness in children than is generally realized. The term *marasmus* is applied to the condition in infants and young children resulting from gross insufficiency of food. Physicians in the tropics and subtropics are all too familiar with the wasted limbs, emaciated body, and wizened features of the marasmic child.

Kwashiorkor describes a wide spectrum of deficiency symptoms in young children caused primarily by a shortage of high-quality protein in the diet. A shortage of calories is often involved as well, though this is not always the case. The word "kwashiorkor" comes from the Ga dialect of West Africa and means literally "first-second," its connotation being "the disease the first child gets when the second is expected," for it is traditionally associated with the post-weaning period and is confined almost entirely to children between the age of weaning and five years. Not until after World War II was it generally agreed that a number of serious disturbances found among young children in Middle and South America, Asia, and throughout tropical Africa were variants of this disease, and that protein malnutrition was its primary cause.

The child suffering from *kwashiorkor* fails to gain weight; he is peevish; his appetite fails. Vomiting and diarrhea are common, and the disease is frequently complicated by gastro-intestinal infections. Other symptoms include swelling of the legs and hands (edema), skin disorders, and patchy bleaching of the hair and skin. Liver damage almost always occurs. Children suffering from advanced *kwashiorkor* die if they do not receive proper medical treatment; those suffering from mild *kwashiorkor* fall easy prey to other diseases, and their mental and physical development is seriously jeopardized.

Moderate *vitamin A deficiency* is widespread in the tropics and subtropics, and severe vitamin A deficiency occurs frequently in Indonesia,

48

southern India, and in parts of east Africa and northeast Brazil. The most tragic effect of severe vitamin A deficiency is damage to the eyes. If the deficiency is not corrected in time, the entire cornea may be destroyed, leaving the victim blind for life. Children aged six months to three years appear to be the most vulnerable. Infantile *beri-beri*, caused by a deficiency of thiamine (vitamin B_1), is reported to be an important cause of mortality among very young children in certain Asian rice-eating countries. *Rickets* is still common among children in north and northeast Africa, the Eastern Mediterranean, and other regions. Rickets is caused by vitamin D deficiency. The action of the sun's rays on the skin leads to the formation of vitamin D. While there is certainly no shortage of sunshine in most of the countries where rickets is still common, the children are frequently kept indoors for most of the day and are carefully bundled up against the sun when they are taken outside.

Among the diseases associated with mineral deficiencies, *anemia* and *endemic goitre* are the most common. Anemia is one of the commonest of all human diseases. While it occurs in all age groups, pregnant and nursing women and growing children are particularly prone to it. Much of the anemia in the tropics and subtropics is caused by, or aggravated by, blood-destroying diseases like malaria and hookworm, but iron-deficiency anemia is also quite common, and protein deficiencies contribute to the disease. Endemic goitre, caused primarily by a deficiency of iodine, is also widespread, but it tends to be more prevalent in mountainous inland regions.

No one is in a position to make even an informed guess concerning the actual number of children who suffer from these various disorders, but we have enough evidence to indicate that undernutrition and malnutrition play an important role in almost all serious illness among pre-school children in the tropics and subtropics. National food balance sheets compiled by FAO reveal that milk and other "protective" foods are in very short supply throughout these regions, and selective dietary and nutrition surveys bear out this presumptive evidence of widespread malnutrition among children, as does a careful study of the available vital statistics. Reduced blood serum albumin, indicating protein deficiency, was observed in 30 to 40 per cent of large samplings of children in four states in southern India in 1956-7. One of the milder forms of *kwashiorkor* is so common in some parts of rural Africa that the irregular bleaching of the hair that accompanies it is considered a normal stage of child development. The mortality rate of children aged one to four in Guatemala is over 40 times higher than in the United States and Western Europe. In the judgment of Dr. Nevin Scrimshaw, former director of the Institute of Nutrition of Central America and Panama, inadequate protein intake is the factor largely responsible.

Undernourished and malnourished children usually live in communities heavily infested with infectious and parasitic diseases. In practice, it is difficult to disentangle the ill effects of these hazards. Seasonal epidemics of dysentery and diarrhea are often followed by outbreaks of deficiency diseases. Almost 100 per cent of the children in many tropical countries are infested with intestinal parasites. Some of the food eaten by these children only nourishes the worms in their intestines; some is lost through diarrhea; and some is poorly assimilated because of other chronic infections. It is generally agreed that malnutrition predisposes to infection and that infection aggravates the effects of malnutrition. Malnutrition warrants special attention because it is such a critical world problem, but it must never be forgotten that nutrition is intimately related to almost every other aspect of public health.

FOOD PRODUCTION AND NUTRITION

A glance at the two accompanying graphs shows that, on the average, the countries with the lowest per caput national income are the very countries where the highest percentage of the male labor force is engaged in agriculture, where the fewest number of calories are available for individual consumption, and where the highest percentage of these calories is derived from starchy staples. The basic difficulty in increasing agricultural production in the technologically underdeveloped countries lies in the fact

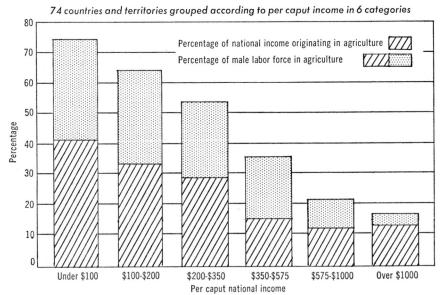

DEGREE OF DEPENDENCE ON AGRICULTURE

74 countries and territories grouped according to per caput income in 6 categories

Source: E/CN.5/346 (p. 108).

50

that the farming community in these countries is far and away the poorest in the world. The great majority of rural inhabitants are subsistence farmers using methods of cultivation that have changed little for centuries.

The very poor quality of the diet that prevails in most of these countries is, like its insufficiency, rooted to a large degree in backward agricultural practices. An undue proportion of food production may be devoted to crops such as cassava, with a high energy value but extremely poor in protein. Even where an effort has been made to modernize agricultural methods, most of it has gone into the production of cash crops for export: sugar, coffee, bananas, cocoa, and the like. The population usually subsists on one or two easy-to-grow starchy staples. Ironically, the very countries where hunger is most prevalent derive the highest percentage of their national income from agriculture because of lack of industrial development.

Logically, the attack on hunger in a given country must be conceived as part of a program of balanced economic and social development. While industry must be expanded so that national income may be raised, agriculture must at the same time be strengthened so that the workers in industry may be adequately fed. Education, modern credit institutions, a proper land tenure system, and efficient food processing, marketing, and distribution arrangements are among the factors that are essential to agricultural development. As industrialization proceeds, agriculture will then benefit from in-

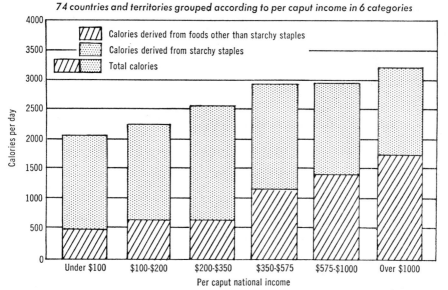

AVERAGE PER CAPUT CONSUMPTION OF FOOD

74 countries and territories grouped according to per caput income in 6 categories

Calories derived from foods other than starchy staples
Calories derived from starchy staples
Total calories

Calories per day

Per caput national income

Source: E/CN.5/346 (p. 108).

creased supplies of fertilizers and farm equipment and a strengthened domestic market for its products.

Something that has become clear in the past twenty years is that the problems of undernourishment and malnutrition should not be left to take care of themselves—or even to catch up later—while other development goals are pursued. At the rate the world's population is presently increasing, production of staple crops will have to be at least doubled by the end of this century; if acceptable levels of nutrition are to be achieved, production of milk, meat, eggs, and fish (or of satisfactory vegetable-protein products) will have to be tripled or quadrupled.

By far the greater part of these production increases will have to take place in the developing countries themselves. Not only are these the countries where present food supplies are the most precarious, they are also the countries where the greatest proportionate population increase is anticipated. The practical difficulties are enormous; but, owing to the inefficient methods of cultivation that presently prevail in these countries, so are the potentials for expanded production, if recent advances in science and technology can be widely exploited. What is needed as a first step in most of the developing countries is a realistically thought-out national food and nutrition policy. This would take into account:

- The nutritional needs of the country's present and anticipated population, including the special needs of children and other vulnerable groups.

- The country's food-producing potential (including the conventional products of its farms and gardens, its off-shore fishing potential, and new resources that might be developed as a result of further scientific research).

- The various economic and social measures that would have to be taken to stimulate (1) the increased production of the kind of foods needed and (2) their increased consumption by the poorly nourished groups of the population.

In general, agricultural development tends to lag behind industrial development. Many of the developing countries have in recent years embarked on extensive programs to redress the balance between these sectors. India, for example, spent a little over $2 billion under its Second Five-Year Plan on agriculture, community development, and irrigation, and plans to spend about $3.5 billion on this sector under its Third Five-Year Plan (1961-6). Large amounts of bilateral aid are contributing to India's efforts along these lines. In the $1 billion worth of loans and grants to which the United States committed itself during the first year of the inter-American "Alliance for Progress," agricultural development figures prominently. Agricultural de-

52

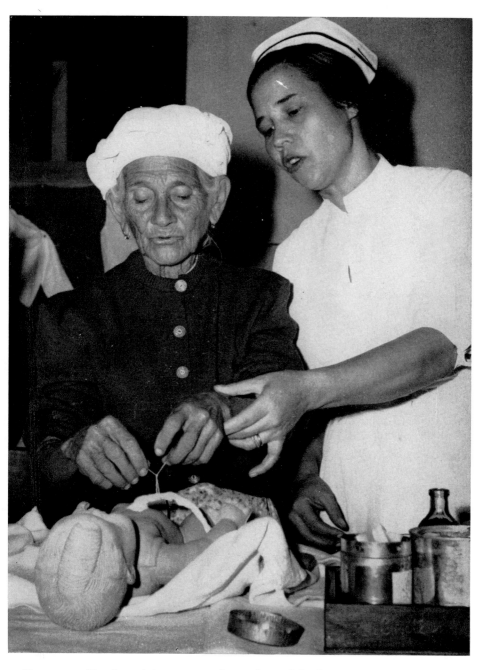

PARAGUAY. Simple training courses for traditional birth attendants help extend better care during childbirth to the many women still beyond the reach of organized government health services.

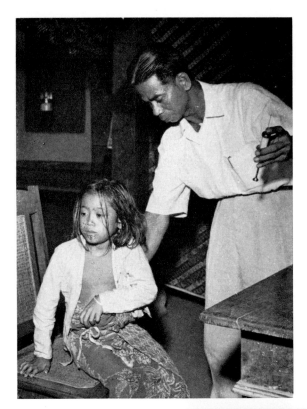

INDONESIA. Some widespread diseases (such as yaws, which has so badly ulcerated this girl's face) can be controlled, or even wiped out, through special mass campaigns. This eases the burden on permanent health services.

INDONESIA. One shot of penicillin has completely healed the same girl in a few weeks. Dramatic results, like this, help mobilize support for further health measures.

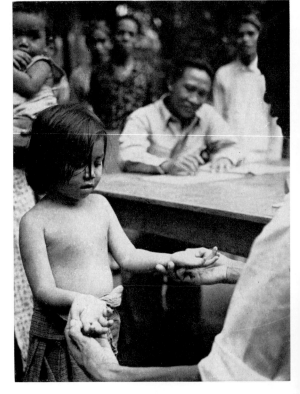

IRAQ. Undernutrition, a polite word for semi-starvation,
is still a much more common
cause of sickness in children
than is generally realized.

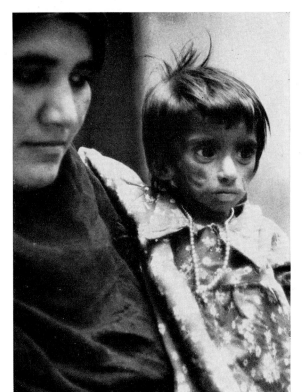

IRAQ. This is the same child
after treatment—mainly plenty
of nourishing food—in a Bag-
dad hospital.

GHANA. In many cultures the breadwinner is served first and gets the best of the available food. Where custom prescribes special foods for young children, these are often bland and starchy.

UGANDA. In southern Uganda, *ettu*—mashed plantain steamed in a plantain-leaf packet—is the traditional weaning food. At Mulago Hospital, mothers are taught to improve their children's nutrition by adding mashed beans or peanuts to the plantain before it is cooked. (Jelliffe photo)

MEXICO. Fish farming is one of the most promising ways of increasing local supplies of animal protein. Fish can be raised in village ponds or even in flooded rice paddies. (UN photo)

velopment also figures in the aid programs of the Colombo Plan countries and the European Common Market countries.

The modernization of agriculture in the developing countries will require decades, even if all goes well. Meanwhile, food surpluses from some of the agriculturally advanced countries are helping to bridge the gap between production and requirements. In recent years, the United States alone has been shipping about a billion and a half dollars worth of surplus foods abroad annually. Some of these surpluses are donated outright to the developing countries and some are sold to them below cost and under arrangements that necessitate no foreign exchange expenditures on their part.

The assistance being channeled through the United Nations and the Specialized Agencies is small relative to the need that exists and, indeed, in comparison with what the agriculturally depressed countries are themselves spending along these lines. This multilateral assistance has, however, made it possible for the governments of the developing countries to benefit from the services of top experts; it has helped them bridge their hard currency gaps, thus opening the way for far greater expenditures of local resources; and it has helped to get important programs under way.

Substantial efforts are now being made to increase the flow of international assistance in the field of food production and nutrition. FAO is sponsoring a special five-year Freedom from Hunger Campaign. The objective of this campaign, which was launched in 1960, has been described by B. R. Sen, the Director-General of FAO, in the following terms:

> It is clear that nothing short of an agricultural revolution in the less developed countries can bring about the changes needed for promoting self-sustained growth. How is this agricultural revolution to be organized and financed? I think our best hope lies in a concerted effort on a world-wide basis in which, not only the United Nations and its Specialized Agencies, but also national governments, non-governmental organizations, religious bodies, foundations, citizens' groups, and men and women of good will everywhere would participate and to which they would contribute their moral and material support. The Freedom from Hunger Campaign has been designed to serve as the focal point for such an endeavor.*

The Freedom from Hunger Campaign is seeking support—from governments, individuals, and private organizations—for a series of national action projects for producing more and better food, getting the food to the people, charting policies and plans, training and education, and strengthening government services. A $100 million, three-year World Food Program in support of the objectives of the Freedom from Hunger Campaign was approved by the United Nations General Assembly in December 1961. In this program, government contributions of surplus foods, cash, and services will

---

*The Basic Freedom—Freedom from Hunger (Rome: FAO, 1960).

be used for relieving acute food shortages, for supplementing the diets of special groups such as children and mothers, and for reinforcing programs of economic development that are likely over the short term to increase the demand for food faster than the agricultural development can be accelerated. The United States has embarked on its own bilateral "Food for Peace" program designed to use surplus foods for similar purposes.

UNICEF's assistance in the field of nutrition, which is now running to more than $7.5 million a year, is planned and executed in close collaboration with FAO and WHO. A recent conference sponsored by the three organizations defined the objective of a sound food and nutrition policy as "the provision of the right kind of food to ensure optimum health and efficiency of the population." The kind of agricultural development whose success can be measured by an increase in the gross tonnage or dollar value of national agricultural production may, indirectly, be stimulated by certain of UNICEF's efforts, but this is not their primary end. The object of UNICEF assistance in this field is specifically to improve the nutrition of the most vulnerable groups in the developing countries, children and mothers—a goal that may only too easily be lost sight of when long-term plans for the development of agriculture are drawn up. The remainer of this chapter is devoted to a brief survey of some of the concrete programs being carried out with international assistance to promote the production and use of the kinds of foods required by growing children and by pregnant and nursing women.

FACT FINDING AND PLANNING

Nutrition programs cannot be planned in the dark, and the dearth of relevant information is one of the greatest difficulties standing in the way of effective action programs in many poorly fed parts of the world. Considerable progress has been made in recent years in developing efficient techniques for carrying out nutrition surveys in less developed areas. Because of the diversity of information that may be pertinent, a survey team, if possible, should include: a physician, to conduct clinical examinations; a nutritionist, to analyze foods and dietary intakes; an agricultural production expert; a food processing technician; and a home economist. One or more laboratory technicians will probably be required and a trained statistician. Since cultural factors play such an important role in determining the kind of food people eat and the kind of food they give their children, an anthropologist will be an invaluable addition to most survey teams. Also included might be a dentist and a pediatrician.

Some of the questions the members of a nutrition survey team will seek to answer are the following:

- What is the extent of malnutrition among children and other vulnerable groups in various areas?

- What deficiencies are involved? How serious is their effect on the people's health and vitality?

- Are local food resources available that could be used to overcome these deficiencies? Are they being overlooked or wasted because of ignorance, dietary prejudices, or the lack of suitable processing, preservation, or distribution facilities?

- If the proper foods are not available, could they be introduced or developed?

How the beginnings of a coordinated national nutrition program can grow out of such a survey may be seen in the case of Ethiopia. Following preliminary surveys by WHO and FAO, a comprehensive Ethiopian nutrition survey was conducted in 1958 by the Ethiopian Government and the United States Interdepartmental Committee on Nutrition. The survey revealed that, while over-all food production in the country was fairly adequate, certain adjustments were needed: for example, greater emphasis on fresh fruits and vegetables in some areas to remedy low vitamin A and C intakes. The survey also found that a better milk supply would be valuable, particularly to improve the nutrition of young children. The greatest needs that the survey revealed were for better food handling, marketing, and storage facilities and for the general education of families in the principles of sound nutrition.

The 1958 survey and the national nutrition conference that followed in 1959 were instrumental in crystalizing the Government's awareness of the country's nutritional problems. Since then the Government has established an interdepartmental food and nutrition board, including representatives from United Nations and bilateral aid agencies. And it has embarked on a concerted program that includes the development of agricultural and home economics extension services as well as the training of elementary school teachers in the fundamentals of nutrition education.

FAO and WHO have assigned experts to assist a number of governments in reviewing their nutritional problems, and UNICEF is now prepared to make grants to governments to help them assess the nutritional needs of their children and draw up long-range plans to meet these needs within the framework of their larger development efforts. The organizational resources of the developing countries are severely limited, but it has been found that, with careful planning, the machinery set up to administer one type of program can frequently be extended to cover others, provided relatively modest additional resources can be found. Measures to improve the nutrition of village and farm families can often be worked in with other efforts to improve rural conditions if one of the considerations regularly guiding planners is a national nutrition policy. An example of this "multipurpose" approach is a UNICEF-assisted regional project in tropical Africa, prepared with the inspiration and help of FAO, to join nutrition education to the training of agricultural extension workers. UNICEF has committed itself to more than $1.3 million worth of aid in connection with this project for the period 1962-4.

MORE FOOD FROM THE LAND

Though in parts of Asia the balance is a precarious one, the developing countries on the whole can at present produce enough food to meet the basic calorie requirements of their populations. They concentrate on high-energy staples—ranging from cereals such as rice, wheat, millet, and maize (which supply appreciable, if not great, amounts of many protective nutrients) to yams, plantain, and cassava (which supply almost nothing except carbohydrates). Because yields are extremely low, there is little land left over for the production of protein-rich and other protective foods to supplement these high-energy staples. So that more land can be devoted to the cultivation of protective foods—and also so that the energy requirements of a rapidly increasing population can be met—yields must be increased as rapidly as possible.

Theoretically, the problem is not difficult. By applying the techniques already in use in Europe, North America, Australia, and Japan, food production throughout the technologically underdeveloped world could be sharply increased without bringing a single new acre under the plough. Extensive use of fertilizers, irrigation, pest control, and the development of improved strains of crops have contributed to a rise in agricultural productivity paralleling the rise in industrial productivity in the technologically developed countries. There is no reason to suppose that appropriately developed scientific methods would not work equally well in the world's less developed areas, where farmers still get little more from their land than did the European peasants of the early Middle Ages. The practical difficulties are immense, however, and in many rural areas nothing short of an economic and social revolution would be required. Nevertheless, beginnings can be made in a number of different ways. An approach worth noting is "rural community development."

One of the important objects of rural community development is to show the people of rural communities how they can grow better crops by changing certain of their traditional methods of cultivation, and how they can improve their conditions of life in other ways by carrying out simple farm and village improvements. The government may provide community development leaders; it may give the villagers better seeds and extend credits for the purchase of fertilizers and farm machinery; it may subsidize well drilling, road building, and other improvements. But the responsibility for carrying out a particular community development project rests with the people themselves. Community development programs have been inaugurated in India, Pakistan, and a number of parts of Africa and the Americas. The results have not been sensational, since the inertia of most rural communities is difficult to overcome, but they have been encouraging.

MORE MILK FOR THE WORLD'S CHILDREN

The problem of increasing production of the so-called "protective foods," particularly those of animal origin, is more complex. Nevertheless, there are a number of ways in which supplies of the vital nutrients needed by young children can be increased and in which better use can be made of existing supplies.

The rapid growth of dairying and industrial milk processing in Europe, North America, Australia, and New Zealand in the first third of the present century probably did more to improve the nutritional status of children and mothers in these countries than any other single development in the field of food and nutrition. Milk is an excellent source of high-quality protein, calcium, and most of the other nutritional elements children need in their years of most rapid growth. World production of milk rose from an estimated 260 million metric tons per year in the mid-1930's to about 339 million metric tons per year by 1960.

However, three-fourths of the world's milk is produced in Europe, the USSR, temperate North America, and Oceania, which regions account for less than a quarter of the world's child population. In India, where milk represents almost the only source of animal protein in family diets, only 50 kilograms of milk per person are available each year as against more than 200 in France and more than 300 in the United States. Furthermore, in all the developing countries milk tends to be a luxury food that the poorer groups find hard to obtain for their children.

In recent years, considerable efforts have been made by countries in the tropics and subtropics to build up milk production and to introduce large-scale industrial processing of milk through the installation of pasteurization, sterilization, and milk drying plants. Preliminary studies have shown that greater resources of milk are available in many of these areas than was previously supposed. Dairying potentials now appear to be good in the countries bordering the Eastern Mediterranean and the Persian Gulf; throughout the eastern portion of Africa, from the Sudan and Ethiopia south to the Cape of Good Hope; and in most parts of Central and South America. In parts of southern and eastern Asia there are promising possibilities as well. Milk from water buffaloes, widely used as draft animals in Asian farming, has provided an important part of the national supply in India, Pakistan, and Iraq. Yet in Thailand, Cambodia, Viet-Nam, and Indonesia these animals are seldom milked.

The governments of the countries concerned have invested important resources in the development of dairying and have been assisted by a number of bilateral and voluntary aid programs as well as by private capital. A considerable amount of aid to dairying has been channeled through the United Nations. FAO has been primarily responsible for providing international assistance to governments in the field of dairy husbandry, which includes all aspects of breeding, management, feeding, and disease control in dairy cattle. UNICEF has concentrated on helping countries where safe milk is hard to procure to introduce the industrial processing of milk. Since 1948 it has been providing imported machinery and equipment, and in many cases engineering assistance, for "milk conservation projects," as they are called, in various parts of the world.

The problem of milk conservation in hot climates is a difficult one. Pasteurization, the classic approach, has worked well in places like Bombay, where facilities for daily collection of milk from farms in the hinterland and for its rapid shipment to and distribution in the city have been successfully developed. But ordinary pasteurized milk spoils quickly if it is not kept under refrigeration. Seasonal surpluses and milk from isolated milk-producing "pockets" may be dried and distributed in powdered form. Drying plants—many of them associated with regular pasteurization and butter-making facilities—in recent years have been established with UNICEF assistance in India, Nigeria, the United Arab Republic, and a number of Central and South American countries.

Another solution coming into increasing favor is to sterilize the milk in hermetically sealed bottles similar to the bottles in which commercial soft drinks are sold. Sufficient pressure is generated in the bottles to keep the milk from boiling, but a temperature of 118°C is maintained long enough to kill all micro-organisms. Sterilized milk keeps indefinitely at room temperatures, provided the seal is not broken. Sterilized milk has a rich, creamy taste, and milk from sterilization plants established with UNICEF assistance in Iraq, Israel, Spain, and Italy has become a popular drink. While the cost of sterilization equipment is higher than that of pasteurization equipment, sterilized milk is cheaper to distribute and store in a hot climate if refrigeration costs are taken into account. Hence, in many tropical areas, sterilization might, in the long run, prove the more economical method of milk conservation.

Annual UNICEF allocations for milk conservation projects averaged $2,122,000 for the period 1961-2. From 1948 to 1962 UNICEF had allocated assistance to milk conservation projects in 35 countries, including 164 fluid milk plants, 33 milk drying plants, and 10 milk institutes, dairy training centers, or schools. When all these plants are in full operation, they will provide, in addition to large quantities of dairy products to be distributed through normal commercial channels, free or subsidized milk for more than 5 million children or mothers in the lower-income groups. The governments aided have been spending on the average more than five times the amounts provided by UNICEF for local capital costs in connection with these projects. In many cases international assistance has been followed by substantial dairy development with private capital.

DRY MILK DISTRIBUTION

While milk production in Asia, Africa, and Central and South America has been steadily increasing since World War II, the increase has been rather slow and in many countries has hardly kept up with population growth. Meanwhile Europe, North America, and Oceania have been producing far more milk than they can consume. So that it may be stored, a large part of this surplus has been converted into dried skim milk.

Skim milk powder (together with a certain amount of whole milk powder) from some of the leading dairy countries has been widely distributed in the less developed countries under various arrangements. In 1959, for example, the United States Government donated 465 million pounds, and the Canadian Government 45 million pounds of surplus dried milk for overseas distribution—equivalent in all to more than 2,500 million liters of liquid milk. These totals included 397 million pounds donated to voluntary agencies for shipment overseas and 99 million pounds donated to UNICEF for shipment overseas. A large part of the surplus milk distributed through the voluntary agencies goes to children and mothers. The voluntary agencies are also taking an increasing interest in school feeding programs.

UNICEF's first work in the field of nutrition was the distribution of skim milk powder, along with other supplementary rations, to the children of war-devastated countries. Since 1951, when UNICEF's mission shifted to long-range programs to aid the children of the less developed countries, relief feeding has of necessity been relegated to a minor position in its nutrition program. UNICEF-supported skim milk distribution programs are now conducted primarily as an adjunct to long-range health and nutrition projects. In 1962, 76 countries were receiving milk for distribution through health centers and schools. The standard ration is one large cup of milk a day—sometimes supplemented by a vitamin A and D capsule—for each child. Experience has shown that the distribution of milk through maternal and child health centers, not only helps overcome deficiencies in the diet of the children affected, but encourages their mothers to bring them in regularly for examination and treatment. Experience has also shown that supplementary feeding accompanied by nutrition instruction in the schools is a valuable means of demonstrating the results of good nutrition to children and their parents and an effective way of stimulating community interest in better nutrition. Basing these programs on imported supplies of surplus powdered milk is no more than a temporary expedient. It is desirable to substitute locally produced milk or other nutritious foods as soon as possible. Frequently, however, the distribution of surplus powdered milk has resulted in such an improvement in child health that national and local governments have been led to embark on extensive milk conservation projects of their own.

Generally UNICEF pays only the ocean freight costs—averaging about 2½ cents a pound—on the dried milk distributed through these programs. The donor country absorbs the costs of production and processing, and the beneficiary country the local distribution costs. By taking full advantage of existing possibilities in this manner, UNICEF has been able to arrange for a growing child in one of the world's less developed areas to receive a full year's supplementary ration of skim milk—about a glass and a half a day—at a cost to the Fund of only 50 cents. About five and one-half million children or nursing mothers are currently benefiting from this part of UNICEF's program.

For 1961 UNICEF shipments of dried milk came to about 100 million pounds. Of this, 96.8 million pounds were dried skim milk donated by the United States Government; 2 million pounds consisted of dried whole milk donated by the Canadian and Swiss Governments; and 575,000 pounds consisted of whole milk powder purchased by the Swiss public through a special "milkday" drive and donated to UNICEF.

It should be noted that dry skim milk, while as good a source of protein and calcium as whole milk, is lacking in vitamin A, normally supplied to infants by the butter fat in the milk they drink. Some 6,700,000 pounds of the skim milk powder shipped by UNICEF in 1961 were fortified with vitamins A and D for use in Indonesia, where vitamin A deficiency is a serious problem among young children.

GREATER PRODUCTION OF OTHER FAMILIAR PROTECTIVE FOODS

Despite the gratifying results of many milk conservation projects in the tropics and subtropics, the prospects of supplying every child with even a third of a liter of milk per day are slight. The immediate obstacle is the high cost of safe milk in relation to family incomes in most parts of the world. Even if this problem could be overcome, there are many areas where it would take decades to build up a reliable milk supply. Fortunately, there are excellent possibilities of increasing production of other familiar protective foods—fish, eggs, garden vegetables, etc.—in almost all the developing countries. Marine fisheries have been little developed along the extensive African and Southeast Asian coastlines. In many places fresh water fish can be raised in flooded rice fields and in village fish ponds. Many of the protective foods so desperately needed by young children can be inexpensively grown in village and home gardens.

Beginning around 1955, UNICEF, FAO, WHO, and various regional, governmental, and private organizations embarked on a "united and expanded effort" to find ways of combatting malnutrition in children—in particular protein malnutrition—through a variety of acceptable foods that might be locally produced at a reasonable cost. Through community development and agricultural extension programs, efforts are now being made in many countries to encourage increased production of familiar protective foods. In many densely populated areas—the State of Uttar Pradesh in India, for example —a greater production of protective foods can be obtained only by growing a second or even a third crop every year, since the first crop is required to meet the population's calorie supply. This procedure usually necessitates the use of irrigation and fertilizers.

An important phase of this campaign is an education program to show villagers in underdeveloped rural areas how they can produce and make better use of common protective foods that require no special processing. A rabbit hutch outside the local school, a village fish pond, a plot of beans in every garden are some of the simple and eminently practical solutions being encouraged. In many villages, too, a considerable number of poultry could be raised if the villagers could be taught to protect their birds against disease.

NUTRITION EDUCATION

The importance of high-protein and other protective foods has to be recognized before people will go out of their way to produce them and feed them to their children. Hence nutrition education is an indispensable part of any campaign to combat malnutrition and a necessary adjunct to all the measures outlined above. It must include an effort to teach parents the basic principles of child nutrition, a general drive to persuade people to make better use of the protective foods already available to them, and an attack on harmful dietary customs. The attack on harmful customs must often be a subtle one, for these may be firmly entrenched in local tradition. Nutrition education must be extended, not only to rural cultivators, but to the inhabitants of the rapidly growing urban areas as well. An important "feedback" effect of nutrition education can be to stimulate the production of more protective foods by increasing the demand for them.

The role of nutrition education emerges most forcefully in the many situations where better use of existing nutritional resources is the key problem. While cheap supplies of foods containing vitamins and mineral elements commonly lacking in children's diets certainly need to be further developed, few countries are so lacking in potential resources of these that an agricultural production problem is involved. (Red palm oil, for example, the richest known source of carotene, the vegetable precursor of vitamin A, is one of the principal export commodities of Indonesia, where vitamin A deficiency eye diseases are thought to be one of the leading causes of blindness among children.) The problem of getting people to give these foods to their children is largely a matter of nutrition education in the widest sense of the word.

UNICEF'S AID TO APPLIED NUTRITION

UNICEF is now allocating over $4 million a year to further the local production of protective foods other than milk and to stimulate nutrition education.

The fundamental objective of this aid to applied nutrition is to improve the nutrition of rural families through foods they themselves can produce. Most of the projects assisted include a number of different activities. Where necessary, preliminary surveys may be conducted to determine the common deficiencies in rural diets and assess the local resources that might be used to counter them. Many projects involve school and community gardens, village fish ponds, poultry raising, home food preservation and storage, and the orientation of agricultural extension work to include some concern with human nutrition.

An increasing amount of aid in this category finances the training of local nutrition, home economics, and agricultural extension personnel, for a shortage of trained personnel is usually one of the major difficulties. Often these projects are tied in with broader community development programs. By 1963, UNICEF aid was going to 55 projects along these lines in 45 countries —16 projects in Africa, 6 in Asia, 6 in the Eastern Mediterranean region, 2 in southern Europe, and 24 in the Americas—and to 1 related inter-regional project. Besides these, UNICEF was assisting projects for nutrition and health education in the primary schools in Upper Volta and Yugoslavia, and the training of teachers in health and nutrition in Chile, Haiti, and Thailand. Nutrition education in the schools is a field in which UNICEF aid is expected to expand rapidly in the next few years.

Most of the applied nutrition projects assisted by UNICEF include a number of different activities. An interesting example is the project undertaken in Bolivia as part of that country's program to improve the condition of its Andean Indians. The project began in 1961 with a survey to determine the dietary habits of the people and the extent of malnutrition among them. Seminars explored the contributions that the doctors, teachers, agricultural experts, and other specialists working on the Andean Indian program could make to the nutrition project. One hundred eighty school teachers are now being trained in the essentials of nutrition, horticulture, small animal raising, and home economics; and about one hundred eighty local auxiliary workers are being trained in home economics. Practical demonstrations in poultry raising, rabbit breeding, and cooking are being carried out in local schools, women's clubs, and "4-H" clubs.

What UNICEF aid means in concrete terms appears in the following list of "UNICEF commitments" for the Bolivian project:

For nutrition surveys: field and laboratory equipment	$10,100
For 37 school gardens: seeds, tools, fertilizers, and pesticides	4,400
For poultry and rabbit raising:	
6 incubators, 12 breeders, wire netting, vaccines, and equipment....	1,800
For home economics: 367 kerosene stoves and equipment	8,000
For audio-visual education:	
film projector, radios, paper, ink, films, and books	6,400
Transport: two vehicles for supervision and survey work	5,300

Total supplies and equipment		$36,000
Freight		$3,650
Stipends:		
30 central supervisors, 2 weeks at $30	$ 900	
25 field supervisors, 4 weeks at $50	1,250	
180 school teachers, 1 month at $45	8,100	
180 indigenous auxiliaries, 1 month at $20	3,600	
stipends for tutorial staff	2,500	$16,350
Total allocation (voted by June 1961 Executive Board)		$56,000

IODIZED SALT

Endemic goitre, caused primarily by the lack of the dietary trace element iodine required in minute amounts by the thyroid gland, is still one of the world's commonest nutritional disorders. Special measures are required to deal with it, since it is associated with iodine-deficient soils rather than with poor diet. In many areas of the developed countries where endemic goitre was once common—the Great Lakes region of North America, for example —the wide distribution of iodized salt has practically eliminated it as a public health problem. WHO's study of endemic goitre has done much to call attention to its continuing prevalence in a number of developing countries. UNICEF has allocated assistance for small-scale salt iodization projects in India, Paraguay, and Thailand, and is aware of the need for goitre-control action in a number of other countries, notably Ethiopia, Lebanon, Pakistan, Indonesia, and Taiwan.

Many problems would be involved in the wide-scale distribution of iodized salt in these countries, for most of their salt is marketed either in the form of moist crystals, obtained from the evaporation of sea-water by sunlight, or rock salt, blasted out of the earth in mining operations. Free-running salt is iodized in Europe and the United States by mixing it with potassium iodide (KI), but this compound will not remain stable in moist salt. A solution developed by WHO is to substitute the more stable potassium iodate (KIO_3). Work is proceeding on the design of a simple rig for adding iodate to a wide variety of crude salts. As a first step toward goitre control, throughout endemic areas, such units could be brought into service in particular localities where the incidence of goitre is highest.

NEW HIGH-PROTEIN FOODS

In recent years an increasing amount of attention has been focused on the development of new high-protein foods, especially high-protein foods suitable for children.

One reason is that population is pressing hard on food supplies in a number of the developing countries. It is not at all certain that production of conventional protective foods can be augmented rapidly enough to meet the needs of the increasing child population.

Another is that there is a great migration to the cities all over the world. Often the new arrivals fare worse in the cities than they did in their native villages, for they are then dependent on foods they can buy cheaply in the market. These consist largely of carbohydrate-rich staples that can be stored in open sacks at room temperature—polished rice, maize meal, cassava, white flour, refined sugar, and the like. Milk, eggs, meat, and other protective foods are luxuries they can seldom afford.

To fulfil the nutritional needs of these new migrants to the city and their children—and, where necessary, to supplement the diet of mothers and children in rural areas—cheap, acceptable, nutritious foods with a long shelf-life must be found. Ideally, these should be foods that can be processed from locally obtainable raw materials not already being widely used for human food. The most promising raw materials appear to be (1) the large potential catches of fish not used as human food because of the lack of suitable processing, transportation, and storage facilities; and (2) the "oil-seed press-cakes"—the protein-rich residues of the extraction of oil from soybeans, peanuts, cottonseed, coconut, and other oil-seeds—now used largely as animal feed or fertilizer.

The search for new high-protein foods received a powerful stimulus in 1956, when the Rockefeller Foundation made the first of two grants, which were to total $550,000, to support laboratory and clinical research along these lines in various parts of the world. UNICEF allocated $100,000 in 1956, and an additional $200,000 in 1959, to support a parallel program of technological and industrial studies, the purpose of which was to get any promising new high-protein product into production as quickly as possible. Guidance for this program is provided by the joint FAO/WHO/UNICEF Protein Advisory Group, an international body of leading nutritionists and pediatricians which meets twice a year to review the latest developments, recommend areas in which further research is needed, and advise the United Nations Agencies on the suitability and safety of new products.

SCIENTIFIC CONSIDERATIONS

Not all proteins have the same nutritive value. In general, animal proteins have a considerably higher nutritive value than plant proteins. The proteins that make up the various human tissues, enzymes, etc. are complex molecules assembled from some 22 simpler compounds known as amino acids. If adequate amounts of 8 of these amino acids are present in the diet, the adult human body can synthesize the rest it needs. These 8 "essential" amino acids must be present simultaneously in certain proportions in the food we eat in order for it to nourish us properly. Young children not only have higher protein requirements than adults, but seem to require a slightly wider selection of amino acids—perhaps 10. The difference in nutritive value between animal and vegetable proteins derives largely from their amino acid composition. Proteins from fruits, vegetables, grains, and nuts supply important amounts of many amino acids, but they do not supply so well balanced an assortment as do animal proteins.

In Europe, the United States, and other technologically advanced areas, scientific research to improve livestock nutrition preceded by some years scientifically oriented efforts to improve the nutrition of children. Fortunately, a great deal of the research carried out on animals has proved directly applicable to human nutrition. Two basic principles long recognized in livestock feeding have a direct bearing on the problem of meeting the protein needs of the world's children:

- The nutritive value of low-quality protein foods can be enhanced by the addition of relatively small amounts of high-quality protein foods.

65

- Low-quality protein foods can be improved by mixing them in prescribed proportions with certain other low-quality protein foods.

The theory of amino acid balancing largely explains these effects. Most animal proteins have essential amino acids to spare; hence, when mixed with vegetable proteins, they tend to make up for the critical deficiencies of the latter. Not all vegetable proteins have the same amino acid deficiencies; hence, if properly mixed, their deficiencies tend to cancel one another out. Essentially, the object of the research and development work that UNICEF and other agencies have been supporting is to find practical, safe ways of applying these principles to infant nutrition.

FISH FLOUR

A cheap, virtually tasteless and odorless high-protein powder would provide an ideal supplement for upgrading the protein value of the foods on which infants are traditionally weaned in many areas. A promising possibility is "fish flour." There is no shortage of raw material here. Owing to storage, transportation, and other problems, only a fraction of the total protein obtained from the sea every year is used for human food. A large part of the rest is now converted into a dehydrated fish meal, widely used as a supplement for fattening livestock in the economically developed countries. Production has boomed in recent years and has outrun demand.

Several processes have been developed in the laboratory to convert fish meal—or freshly caught fish—into a light gray flour, measuring up to the most exacting hygienic and biological standards. These fish flours contain 70 to 80 per cent protein of a high nutritive value, and can be incorporated in small amounts into bread, or added to soups and stews, without appreciably affecting their taste. About 20 grams a day of such fish flour added to the food of a child in the critical one- to five-year age group should meet his protein requirements. Preliminary estimates indicate that this amount of fish flour might not cost more than one cent to produce.

A number of fish flour pilot plants have been built in various countries by private firms or government agencies. A 300-ton per year fish flour plant has been built at Quintero, Chile, with UNICEF assistance. The results of the Chilean operation will be available for the guidance of any government or private concern interested in undertaking large-scale production of fish flour, and it is now considered merely a matter of time until one or more satisfactory and economic processes are perfected to make this nutritious protein supplement widely available.

The soybean, which by weight contains about 40 per cent protein, has long been regarded as the world's most promising source of vegetable protein. The rich animal protein diet of the United States, now the world's leading soy producer, is firmly rooted in soy-based livestock feeds. Soy is of particular interest to persons concerned with infant nutrition because soy protein, if properly processed, appears to be the only widely available vegetable protein that by itself adequately meets the nutritional requirements of infants and young children. The question of processing is an all-important one, however, for the soybean contains a factor that retards the growth of young animals. This factor is destroyed by the application of the proper amount of heat. Maximum nutritive value of soybean protein is obtained by exact adjustment of temperature, pressure, moisture content, and duration of heating. Good possibilities of increased soy production exist in many parts of the tropics and subtropics, but if soy preparations are to contribute significantly to the elimination of protein malnutrition among young children, not only the cultivation of soybeans, but the development of an appropriate processing technology must be encouraged in these regions.

About 600 tons a year of Saridele, a vegetable milk powder based on four parts of soybean extract to one part of sesame seed extract, are now being turned out at a plant near Jogjakarta, Indonesia, completed in 1957 with UNICEF assistance. There are as yet virtually no local supplies of cow's milk in Indonesia, and soybean derivatives are considered the best immediate hope of eliminating protein malnutrition among Indonesian children. However, present Saridele production is equivalent to a milk production of only about 15,000 liters a day. The product, though it sells at about half the price of imported cow's milk, is still too expensive for unsubsidized use by low-income families. Another possibility being explored is *tempeh*—fungus-digested soybeans—already prepared by traditional methods in parts of Indonesia. Other traditional methods of soy processing, as practiced in Japan, Taiwan, and other parts of the Far East, are also being investigated.

Meanwhile, significant advances have been made in soy technology in countries like the United States, and the chances of transferring some of this technology to the tropics and subtropics appear favorable. Refined soy products are being increasingly used in the United States in processed foods for human consumption, including commercial baby foods and low-calorie dietary mixtures.

UNICEF has made several grants in an effort to find ways of reducing costs and standardizing the quality of processed soy products. It has awarded a contract to a large commercial producer of soy products to see whether some of the soy preparations now being produced on a mass scale for animal

67

feeding can be adapted to human use without further extensive processing. The prospects are extremely encouraging. Good progress has recently been reported in developing cheap, edible soy flours. In the near future, it is hoped, it will be possible to prepare infant foods based on soy flour at a cost considerably less than that of producing the more complicated "soy milks" like Saridele, or the commercial baby foods now on the market.

COTTONSEED FLOUR MIXTURES

One reason soy flour is so attractive economically is that it can be produced from the protein-rich "press-cake," a by-product of soy oil extraction. Other oil-seed press-cakes—cottonseed, peanut, coconut, palm nut, sunflower seed, and sesame seed—are also rich in protein and are potential resources of great value. None of the flours prepared from these other oil-seed press-cakes is an entirely adequate source of protein by itself, but all have proved their value in various mixtures.

The encouraging results obtained with cottonseed flour are of particular interest since cotton is an important cash crop in many areas where protein malnutrition is prevalent. Cottonseed protein appears to have a very favorable amino acid pattern for supplementing cereal proteins. The Institute of Nutrition of Central America and Panama (INCAP), in Guatemala, has developed a weaning food, sold under the trade name "Incaparina," consisting of four parts of cottonseed flour, three parts maize flour, and three parts sorghum flour, fortified with Torula yeast (to supply vitamins of the B complex), calcium carbonate, and vitamin A. None of the three major ingredients yields a satisfactory protein alone; mixed in these proportions, however, they have proved almost as effective as skim milk in treating *kwashiorkor*. Incaparina can be used to make a thin gruel resembling the maize meal *atole*, the traditional weaning food of the Central American highlands. By the spring of 1961, commercial firms in Guatemala, El Salvador, and Colombia had been licensed to produce and market Incaparina at a price not to exceed four cents for a 75-gram package, nutritionally equivalent to about three cups of milk.

A special conference on cottonseed flour, sponsored by the United States Department of Agriculture, UNICEF, and the cottonseed products industry, was held in New Orleans in November 1960. It now appears that cottonseed flour can be mixed with a variety of cereals to obtain satisfactory high-protein supplements. It also seems fairly certain that, with proper selection of seeds and with reasonably good plant management, it will be possible to produce a satisfactory cottonseed flour in many parts of the world.

PEANUT FLOUR AND OTHER NEW PRODUCTS

Peanuts are widely grown in Africa and southern Asia. India alone produces one-third of the world's peanuts, but a large part of the crop is processed in inefficient village presses that do not extract all of the oil and leave a press-cake that quickly turns rancid. The rancid press-cake cannot be used even for animal fodder, and is either dumped on the fields as fertilizer or, worse, burned. The technology of producing edible peanut flour has now reached an apparently satisfactory stage of development. UNICEF has provided equipment for two peanut flour plants in India and has supported field trials of a peanut flour/milk mixture in Nigeria. Studies carried out in England, Nigeria, and India have shown that a mixture of 80 per cent peanut flour and 20 per cent skim milk powder supports growth in children as efficiently as milk alone. In programs relating to peanut flour, as in all high-protein food programs, care has to be taken to ensure that only sound raw materials are used and that they are properly processed and handled.

Work has commenced on obtaining edible protein-rich preparations from coconut, sesame seed, and sunflower seed. UNICEF and the Protein Advisory Group are following with close interest experiments in a number of laboratories to obtain high-protein concentrates from leaves, grasses, yeasts, and algae. The possibilities of supplementing certain diets with synthetic amino acids is also being explored. It is believed, however, that the largely unexploited resources of low-quality fish and oil-seed press-cakes offer better hope for the immediate future than these more exotic possibilities.

GETTING INTO PRODUCTION

If some of the more important answers to the technical problems involved in developing new high-protein foods have been found, the remaining problems of adapting these solutions to local conditions and applying them where they are most needed, is an equally challenging one. To this the international agencies are giving increasing attention. A basic need is the training of local food technologists. In June 1961, the UNICEF Executive Board decided to extend its aid to nutrition training to the field of food science and technology. An example of such aid is a cooperative arrangement that has been worked out between UNICEF and the United States Department of Agriculture, whereby UNICEF pays the fellowship costs for research trainees from some of the less developed countries to work on the Department's soy and cotton-seed utilization projects.

Considerable effort is also being made to encourage commercial firms with experience in promotion and marketing, to join the campaign to get high-protein food supplements into normal channels of distribution. While UNICEF,

FAO, and WHO channel their assistance through governments, their program is flexible enough to permit effective cooperation with private industries within a country, to the mutual advantage of all concerned.

A COOPERATIVE ACHIEVEMENT

Close cooperation among various international, national, and private bodies will be required to get the new high-protein foods into mass production so that they may be made available to the mothers and children who need them most, but this will be merely an extension of that which has existed since the search for these foods began.

Most of the laboratory experiments have been conducted by privately endowed or government supported universities and hospitals. Many outstanding chemists, nutritionists, and pediatricians have contributed their time and effort, often without pay. Dairy industry groups have cooperated closely with UNICEF on its milk conservation program, and so have groups in the fish meal, soy, and cottonseed industries in the high-protein food program. Indeed, only a small part of the necessary financial support and workload has been supplied directly by UNICEF and the other United Nations agencies.

The importance of the UNICEF/FAO/WHO contribution is that it has been the first systematic attempt to coordinate world-wide scientific efforts to deal with the problem of protein foods for children in the developing countries. The results achieved, incomplete as they may be, are impressive enough to demonstrate the value of international cooperation to enlist science and the industrial arts in the fuller service of humanity.

CHAPTER IV
Education and Vocational Training

CHILDREN WHO SURVIVE to the age of six or seven have surmounted the greatest hazards of disease and malnutrition. Thereafter they enter on a period of relative stability so far as their health is concerned.

At this point their greatest need is education. Without it, the children of the less developed countries can do little, when adults, to improve their precarious living conditions. Yet a large proportion of them have no opportunity to acquire the most fundamental knowledge and skills that would prepare them to deal with the changing world they live in. In 1957-8, in the less developed part of the world as a whole, only one-half of the children of primary school age were in school.

The right to an education is clearly expressed in the Universal Declaration of Human Rights, which states that education should be free, "at least in the elementary and fundamental stages;" elementary education should be "compulsory," technical and professional education "generally available," and higher education "equally accessible to all on the basis of merit." All states accept this "right to education" as a principle of public policy, and all governments are striving to make sufficient provisions for the education of their children. In the developing countries, the recognition that more and better schooling is the *sine qua non* of economic and social progress lends additional urgency to these efforts.

There has been considerable progress over the past ten years in extending education to a greater proportion of the world's children. In the Arabic-speaking countries, for example, between 1950 and 1960 primary school attendance doubled, secondary school attendance tripled, and higher education attendance doubled. But we are still far from the goals set forth in the Declaration of Human Rights. The following table gives the latest available school enrolment figures for the world and its component regions.

This table reveals a striking contrast between the situation in the high-income regions (Europe, North America, Oceania, and the USSR) and the low-income regions (Africa, Asia, Middle and South America). In the former, about 17.5 per cent of the total population is enrolled in school; in the latter about 10.2 per cent—and this despite the fact that children of

71

ESTIMATED SCHOOL ENROLMENT BY LEVEL, 1957/58

Region	Estimated enrolment by level (thousands)				Estimated total population mid-1957 (thousands)	Total enrolment as percentage of total population
	Primary	Secondary	Higher	Total		
World Total	**260,526**	**70,939**	**9,988**	**341,453**	**2,756,057**	**12.4**
Africa	15,209	1,429	128	16,766	232,569	7.2
North America	31,539	9,750	3,085	44,374	188,682	23.5
Middle and						
South America	21,669	2,769	505	24,943	190,952	13.1
Asia	126,866	26,211	2,460	155,537	1,511,608	10.3
Europe	46,076	16,639	1,642	64,357	413,985	15.5
Oceania	2,168	612	69	2,849	14,661	19.4
USSR	16,999	13,529	2,099	32,627	203,600[a]	16.0

Source: UNESCO, "World Survey of Education," Vol. 3.
[a] Unofficial estimate.

school age account for a substantially larger proportion of the population in the low-income regions. (Children aged five through fourteen account for roughly 20 per cent of the world's population, the general range in the high-income countries being 13-19 per cent and in the low-income countries 22-27 per cent.)

The table also indicates the poor balance between various levels of schooling in the developing countries. In the high-income regions, taken as a group, secondary schools account for 28 per cent of total school enrolment, higher education for 5 per cent. In the low-income regions, secondary education accounts for 10 per cent of total enrolment, higher education for 1 per cent. The low ratios of secondary enrolment to primary enrolment characteristic of the low-income regions (1 to 5 in Asia, 1 to 8 in Latin America, and 1 to 11 in Africa) highlight a major problem: the shortage of facilities to develop the capacities awakened in a large proportion of primary school children. Not all children profit from a secondary education of the classic grammar school kind, but most can profit from some type of secondary schooling. Excessive competition tends to develop among the students as to which ones will be admitted to the available places in secondary school, and psychological tensions, possibly disastrous to the child, may result.

EDUCATIONAL PRIORITIES

Certain regional priorities in the field of education have been suggested at recent UNESCO-sponsored conferences. The representatives of the Asian

SCHOOL ENROLMENT PER 10,000 POPULATION, 1957-1958

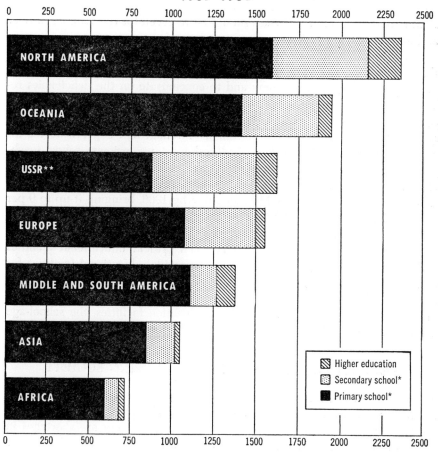

Source: UNESCO *World Survey of Education*, Vol. 3.
*Definition of primary and secondary years not same in all school systems.
**Estimate of total population unofficial.

countries, meeting in Karachi, decided that their essential regional objective should be to eliminate illiteracy and provide all children with a practical education. In Beirut, the representatives of the Arabic-speaking countries called for efforts to ensure balanced educational development, with particular attention to better teaching, the education of girls and women, strengthening secondary education and professional training, and providing more school buildings. The ministers and directors of education of the African countries, meeting in Addis Ababa, decided that at this stage of development a substantial portion of their resources should be reserved for the training of high and middle echelon cadres.

It is becoming the practice in national development planning to assess the output from the various levels of the educational system against the personnel needs of the economy and to concentrate on the deficiencies revealed. The weakness of secondary education in the developing countries is receiving increasing attention, because this weakness is responsible for a fatal shortage of intermediate personnel—foremen and supervisors for industrial and commercial work, agricultural assistants, primary school teachers, nurses and technicians to staff health and welfare services. A Conference of African States on Education, held in 1961, recommended that enrolment in the secondary schools should be doubled by 1966, bringing it up to 9 per cent of that age group; and that primary school enrolment should be increased by one-third, bringing it up to 50 per cent of that age group.

In addition to closing the gap between present educational facilities and needs, the developing countries must provide educational facilities for additional numbers of children as their populations increase. In south and southeast Asia, for example, where, according to a recent UNESCO estimate, 87 million children still lack elementary education facilities, the school-age population is expected to increase by 130 million by 1980.

EDUCATION FOR LIFE IN A DEVELOPING SOCIETY

The quality of the instruction available to the children of the developing countries fortunate enough to attend school leaves much to be desired. There are too few teachers and too few school buildings. There are shortages in school books, other teaching aids, and school furniture. Because the quality of teaching is often poor, the educational process tends to be ineffective, as indicated by the characteristic piling up of pupils in grades one and two, with a high percentage of drop-outs thereafter.

Often the type of education available to the children of the developing countries is poorly adapted to their psychology and environment. Such aspects of education as vocational training, health instruction, and civic consciousness are frequently overlooked. The traditional academic curriculum of these countries tends to turn out clerks, and there are far more applicants for minor white-collar jobs than there are openings. There is now a widespread movement to give a more practical orientation to formal schooling, so as to prepare children to deal with the actual environment they will eventually face.

Through practical instruction in agriculture, crafts, home economics, science, health, and nutrition, the schools can equip a child with the knowledge and skills necessary for him to play a useful role in the economic and social development of his country. As important, perhaps, are the attitudes and habits the child must acquire at school if he is to function effectively in a developing society. This is particularly true in a society whose economic basis is shifting from subsistence farming to industry. As Professor W. A. Lewis, Principal of the University College of the West Indies, has observed:

> An industrial system makes demands on human personality rather different from those made by farming on one's own.
>
> For example, the rhythm of work is different. In agriculture one has short bursts of intense activity from dawn till dusk, associated with planting or with harvesting, followed by long periods of idleness or leisurely activity, in the seasons unfavorable to agriculture. In industry, on the other hand, one is expected to work at an even pace for eight or nine hours every day, for five or six days of every week. Nobody likes this: it is a discipline which one has to acquire.
>
> Again, on the farm, one works as one's master, in a variety of activities, making numerous decisions. In the factory one works under supervision, doing exactly what one is told to do, and acting merely as a cog in some very complicated mechanism, making perhaps one knows not what, to sell to almost certainly one knows not whom. An industrial community is a much more complicated organism than a farming community; more deeply intertwined, yet more impersonal. One has to learn how to find one's way.
>
> Greater precision is demanded in industrial life. The exact hour of the day never matters on the farm; clocks were invented in towns. Time is of the essence of many industrial processes, and new habits of punctuality must be learned. In dealing with nature, too, precision is not so important. If one damages a tree, it will heal itself. If one forgets to feed an animal, it will protest, and even if it misses a meal, this does no great harm. In industry, on the contrary, if measurements are not precise, the parts do not fit; if bolts are not tightened, they fall off. The penalties of carelessness are much greater, and it is much more important to have a sense of personal responsibility for everything that one does.[*]

"Much thought," Lewis concludes, "has been given to adapting school curricula to technical needs, but less thought has been given to how the schools might be used to help young people acquire the attitudes which industrial life requires."

[*]W. Arthur Lewis, "Education and Economic Development," *Final Report; Conference of African States* (UNESCO/ED/181, pp. 71-79).

The physical obstacles to an expansion of the educational system in most developing countries are a limited capacity for teacher training, a shortage of buildings and equipment—particularly at the secondary level at which laboratories and workshops are required—and a shortage of texts and other teaching materials. Classes in which all the pupils share a single textbook are not rare.

To overcome these material obstacles, greater financial resources must be found. The development of education may be correctly considered an investment program. It is one of the most costly of such programs, and it is not usually financed by internationally bankable loans. To attain their announced five-year goal of providing schooling for 50 per cent of primary school-age children, 9 per cent of secondary school-age children, and 0.2 per cent of those of higher education age, the states of the continent of Africa will, it is estimated, have to devote 4 per cent of their national incomes to central and local government outlays for education. To attain their 1980 goal of 100 per cent enrolment at the primary, 23 per cent at the secondary, and 2 per cent at the higher level, they will have to devote 6 per cent of the national income to education. A fully developed education system may require 8 per cent of a country's national income for its financing. The fact that total government revenues presently do not come to 8 per cent of the national income in some underdeveloped countries shows what a difficult task the proper financing of education will be.

The 1960 Report of the Commission on Post-School Certificate and Higher Education in Nigeria, entitled *Investment in Education,* stresses the importance of meeting these goals despite the financial difficulties involved —not merely for the sake of the children affected but for the sake of the future development of their countries.

> To approach our task . . . we have to think of Nigeria in 1980: a nation of some 50 million people, with industries, oil, and a well developed agriculture . . . a nation which is taking its place in a technological civilization, with its own airways, its organs of mass-communication, its research institutes.
>
> Millions of the people who will live in this Nigeria of 1980 are already born. Under the present educational system more than half of them will never go to school. Like people elsewhere, their talents will vary from dullness to genius. Somehow, before 1980, as many talented children as possible must be discovered and educated if this vision of Nigeria is to be turned into reality. This is a stupendous undertaking. It will cost large sums of money. The Nigerian people will have to forego other things they want so that every available penny is invested in education. Even this will not be enough. Countries outside Nigeria will have

to be enlisted to help with men and money. Nigerian education must for a time become an international enterprise.*

What is true of Nigeria is true of all the developing countries. If the educational needs of the world's children are to be met within the next thirty years, the development of education in the world's low-income countries must for a time become an international enterprise. National resources and international resources, the latter to include all available forms of multilateral and bilateral aid, public and private alike, must be mobilized to the fullest possible extent. The present flow of international assistance to education is not sufficient and will need to be increased many fold.

UNITED NATIONS ASSISTANCE

UNESCO is the United Nations agency responsible for common planning, the setting of standards, and the exchange of technical assistance in the field of education. UNESCO does not, however, have the resources to supply large-scale material assistance for teacher training, textbook production, and the like. UNICEF, working in close cooperation with UNESCO, is now moving into this area.

UNICEF's first assistance to education was restricted to health and nutrition education. The Executive Board's decision in June 1961 to extend UNICEF assistance to acceptable projects having to do with any of the high-priority needs of children opened the way for broader assistance to education. In 1962 the Board approved commitments totalling $4,600,000 for 14 education projects in 12 countries: Bolivia, Brazil, Congo (Leopoldville), Indonesia, Iran, Iraq, Lebanon, Libya, Peru, Thailand, Tunisia, and Yugoslavia. Teacher training is an important feature of all these projects. The objective is, not only to train more teachers, but to train them in the practical subjects that need to be added both to primary and secondary schooling in these countries. In Tunisia, for example, the primary school curriculum has been completely revised since 1958, but the teaching of practical subjects still lags because few teachers have more than a sketchy knowledge of these subjects. It will take at least five years to familiarize enough Tunisian teachers with the new approach for the revised curriculum, based on the philosophy of "practical preparation for life," to be generally introduced.

The Brazilian project is a notable instance of the kind of cooperative effort needed for the educational problems of the developing countries to be solved in the foreseeable future. The underdeveloped states of Mato Grosso, Goias, and Paraiba have been selected for this project. In these states less than 26 per cent of school-age children attend school. Only 13 per cent of the children who start the four-year primary course in urban areas complete

---

* *Investment in Education* (Lagos, Nigeria: Federal Ministry of Education, 1960).

it, and only 5.6 per cent of those who start the three-year primary course in rural areas complete it. Each of these states is establishing an educational planning commission, and the Federal Government of Brazil expects to spend $1,600,000 to assist their teacher training programs. UNESCO is providing extensive technical assistance to the project, and the United States Agency for International Development (AID) is helping train key personnel. UNICEF has committed itself to $657,000 worth of aid over a period of three years, including supplies and equipment, transport, salaries for experts, and stipends for trainees.

VOCATIONAL TRAINING AND GUIDANCE

Even with the greatest foreseeable expansion of educational facilities, only a small proportion of children in the developing countries can, for years to come, complete secondary school, and only a handful will proceed to higher education. The others will leave school at various ages to join the labor force. To benefit from the employment opportunities that can be expected to open up in a developing economy, and to supply the manpower needs of that economy, they will need vocational training and guidance. Once at work, they will need further on-the-job training and guidance, so that they can advance as they acquire experience.

From the standpoint of the individual, vocational training and guidance are the final stages in the protective care due the child—and later the adolescent—on account of his immaturity and vulnerability. From the standpoint of society, they are the final stages in its investment in the rising generation. If these final stages are well provided for, the economy will receive a stream of young productive workers, trained to meet its specific manpower requirements. Thus society will begin to receive returns on the earlier investments made by parents in caring for their children and by the state through its expenditures on schools and on health and social services for children. The adolescent will then be in a position to take his place in the community as a self-supporting citizen, performing satisfactory and useful work. Later he will be able to support his wife and children properly and help give the next generation a good start in life.

Such is the ideal state of affairs. The actual state of affairs is far different. Work and its problems start at an early age in the developing countries. The minimum legal age for admission to employment ranges from twelve to sixteen in different countries, but it is not always enforced; indeed, in rural areas it is seldom enforced at all. From 2 to 10 per cent of the labor force consists of children under fifteen; over 20 per cent of the labor force consists of "youth," aged fifteen to nineteen. About 80 per cent of male youths are in the labor force; many girls of this age are also working or looking for work, though the proportion is much lower. In Asia and Africa, the youth population is growing by 2 per cent a year; and in South America, by 3 per cent. The following is a description by the Director-General of the International Labour Organisation of what awaits the child or adolescent entering the labor market for the first time:

> Despite all the progress made in recent years—and there has been much—the mid-twentieth century youth has little better than a 50 per cent chance of obtaining any education at all. If he is in the lucky half of the world's young people, he will have gone to school until he is about twelve or fourteen. . . . He may not find a job on leaving school—his chances are especially slim in a country suffering from any appreciable amount of unemployment—and he is about twice as likely as an adult to lose his job. If he has been lucky enough to find a job, the chances are about even that it will be suitable for him; in many cases he will take the first he can get. He is rather less than more likely to have any systematic opportunities for developing his skills and capacities during working hours or to have any real chance of doing this in what free time he may have. He is growing fast in every way and yet lacking in positive health supervision and in constructive outlets for his bursting energies. He is probably working a 48-hour week or so, with little or no control of overtime (whether paid or unpaid), and entitled to two-weeks' holiday per year, which he may or may not feel free to take. He is receiving little responsible help from the adult community in adjusting himself constructively either to work life or to social and civic life. He is apt to be plagued by doubts as to his own status and usefulness in all these spheres.*

YOUTH AND WORK

In the developing countries an increasing number of youths are migrating to urban centers in search of jobs in trade and industry. They represent one of the growing potential resources of the economy, but a resource that cannot be effectively realized unless they receive proper vocational training and guidance. In practice, their potential contribution is largely wasted. Many of these young migrants, lacking the skills in demand, fail to find work. Plunged into an urban fringe environment without legitimate means of subsistence, they tend to drift into delinquency.

The vocational needs of those who remain in their native villages to follow the occupations of their parents in agriculture, handicrafts, and cottage industries also deserve special attention. The young persons who are to enter these traditional employments generally receive no vocational training beyond what their families can provide. Yet, in overpopulated areas, increased agricultural production can be obtained only by raising agricultural

---

* *Report of the Director-General* (Report I), International Labour Conference, 44th Session. "Youth and Work" (Part I) International Labour Organisation, Geneva, 1960.

yields per unit of land. Better trained and better informed cultivators are needed.

Economic factors dominate this unhappy picture. Economic necessity forces handicraft industries to subsist on cheap child labor. The need for money to meet family necessities forces many parents to put their children to work when they should still be attending school. A more rapid rate of economic development would help alleviate the problem of premature employment. It would also result in more and better job opportunities for young persons who have reached a suitable age to work.

Yet economic measures alone will not solve the problems of "youth and work," as the ILO has termed this field. Important social factors are also involved. There is an all too common tendency in the developing countries to regard education as a means of escaping from manual work, rather than as preparation for the work which needs to be done. All too frequently, the kind of education available amounts primarily to a preparation for a government clerkship rather than for technical or professional work. As a result, a considerable body of "educated unemployed" may be found in countries suffering from crippling shortages of supervisory and technical personnel.

The importance of social development to economic development is clearly apparent in this context. Important non-economic measures can help increase the flow of suitably qualified young workers into the sectors of the economy where they are needed. Priority can be given to the expansion of those branches of the educational system whose graduates, according to manpower requirement forecasts, will be most urgently needed. The content and tone of primary and secondary education can be altered to prepare students for manual and technical work. Vocational training can be provided both for students leaving primary school and those leaving secondary school; some of these might work part-time while they are being trained. Vocational guidance and youth placement centers can help direct young workers into the jobs for which they are best suited and where they can make their most effective contribution to the economy.

The needs of youth itself, in relation to work and preparation for work, have been summarized as follows by the Director-General of the ILO:

- The need for a good general education and appropriate training before starting work.
- The need for work.
- The need for development and learning at work.
- The need for special health protection up to at least the age of eighteen.
- The need for leisure.
- The need for confidence in society and its future.

Some of these needs call for special social measures beyond those just suggested: minimum age and hours legislation, health protection at work, etc. Special measures of social protection are required for working mothers. Better provision is necessary for the care of the young children of working mothers.

INTERNATIONAL ASSISTANCE IN THE FIELD OF "YOUTH AND WORK"

Over the past 40 years the ILO has secured the adoption of international conventions dealing with the minimum age at which children may work, the conditions of employment for young workers, and the protection of mothers and pregnant women at work. The ILO also provides governments with technical advice and assistance for vocational services. The organization believes that experimentation with new measures as well as a greater volume of international support is necessary:

> The critical stage is the post-primary stage of education. In most of the developing countries . . . the great mass of the youngsters start their work lives or start seeking work with little or nothing behind them in the way of information about work and jobs, without even the simplest of vocational skills and with little or no knowledge of the employment needs and opportunities of their countries and communities.
>
> The problem is to find a means of giving these children and young people, most of whom are thrown into the employment market at a very early age, some simple, realistic opportunities for finding out what they can do in relation to employment needs and work possibilities, for learning to do it (not with formal skill but with reasonable competence), for moving into work as openings arise, and for developing their capacities to the extent possible once they are in employment. It is not an easy task to find a coordinated means of meeting these basic and interrelated needs, especially given the framework of family poverty within which the solutions must be sought. Yet many aspects of the future of national development will depend on the extent to which these needs for youth vocational development are met.

UNICEF's assistance in the field of vocational services began in 1962 when the Executive Board approved commitments totalling a little more than $1 million in support of projects planned with the help of ILO in four countries: Chile, Costa Rica, Haiti, and Tunisia. In Chile, UNICEF is providing equipment and tools for four youth vocational training centers in one of the large slums on the outskirts of Santiago. Masonry, carpentry, metal work, plumbing, and other building trade skills are being stressed, since the Government has embarked on an extensive housing program in this area. The aim of the Costa Rican project is to provide young people unable to attend regular trade schools with on-the-job training in private industry through government supported and supervised apprenticeship arrangements. In Haiti, the emphasis is on training young people in rural areas to be better farmers. UNICEF is providing equipment for workshops where youths between the ages of twelve and eighteen will be taught such skills as the manufacture of simple agricultural implements, blacksmith work, welding, and basic horticulture.

The most ambitious of these projects is the Tunisian. Here, by 1967, the Government proposes to establish a total of 125 pre-vocational training centers *(centres de pré-apprentissage)* for the benefit of children who have dropped out of school by the age of fourteen. These centers will be of four types:

- Urban centers for boys, offering training in metal work, woodwork, and electricity.

- Maritime centers, where boys will be trained for the fishing industry.

- Rural centers for boys, offering training in agriculture, horticulture, and construction.

- Rural centers for girls, offering training in home economics and care of children.

The Tunisian Government plans to spend the equivalent of $7 million over the next five years to staff, equip, and operate these centers. UNICEF has pledged itself to $800,000 worth of assistance, which will take the form of supplies, equipment, transport, expert's salaries, and stipends for future instructors and vocational counsellors during their training period.

CHAPTER V
Family and Child Welfare

Social change is a necessary concommitant of economic development. Economic development must be vigorously promoted if there is to be any lasting progress in dealing with the ills of children discussed in the previous chapters of this report: sickness, malnutrition, inadequate schooling, and the prospect of a life of poorly paid and unrewarding work—if work can be found.

If would therefore be idle to regret the breakdown of traditional ways of life in the developing countries. But in a period of rapid transition, when there has not been time for the development of a new social framework to replace the traditional one, the individual may find himself trapped in a social vacuum, lacking the protection and support of either traditional or modern patterns of social existence.

Special measures are needed in all the developing countries to ease this difficult period of transition, especially in the field of family and child welfare. The adult can sometimes afford to wait a few years for things to improve, but the growing child cannot. In that time the damage to his social development will have been accomplished.

Nor is the need for new measures of social protection restricted to the period of transition. The developing countries are inevitably moving toward a society based on increasing division of labor and an advancing technology. This implies a new ordering of human relationships, which will dominate life in the cities and whose eventual impact will be great even in remote rural areas.

In this kind of society the individual's relation to the social and economic order to which he contributes his work, and which in return provides him with the necessities of existence, is likely to be a rather impersonal one. The community to which he is responsible, and to which he must turn for protection against the common hazards of life, will no longer be the village, the clan, or the tribe; it will be a political entity embracing thousands or millions of persons. In such a society, mutual aid arrangements no long function automatically or in accordance with customary rules reinforced by centuries of tradition. Social welfare, therefore, becomes a new and continuing *public* responsibility, and one that can be met only by the community at large acting through government channels, cooperative bodies, voluntary agencies, or some combination of these.

SOCIAL CHANGE IN RURAL AREAS: TROPICAL AFRICA AS AN EXAMPLE

Nowhere is the pace of social change more rapid than in the newly independent or soon to be independent countries of tropical Africa. What is happening in tropical Africa in this regard is a dramatic example of what is happening and has been happening—though usually at a less precipitate pace—in most other parts of the tropics and subtropics.

The traditional cultures of tropical Africa, for all their diversity, had certain salient characteristics in common. The population was dispersed among small villages living by subsistence agriculture. Living standards were low, and levels of nutrition and sanitation precarious. The family, village, and tribal community dominated all aspects of existence. But while the individual was rigorously subordinated to the community, he obtained from it a measure of security and a guarantee of group support. Traditional institutions, well enough adapted to a static environment, have tended to disintegrate in the face of the far-reaching political and economic changes accelerated by the coming of the Europeans. These proceeded with gathering momentum under the impact of modern technology, as the spirit of nationalism developed and as independence was attained.

The opening up of roads and railways, the introduction of money, the demand for seasonal labor to harvest export crops, the spread of new ideas —all have led to an increasing mobility among rural populations. The habit of travelling has spread. Money has made it possible for the individual to claim his share of the group heritage to use as he wishes. Wage labor has made it possible for him to sell his services as an individual. Seasonal labor migrations have broadened the villager's perspective and broken down his cultural isolation.

The modernization of agriculture, now regarded as an important aspect of economic development throughout the tropics and subtropics, will inevitably entail a further weakening of traditional ways of life. Land reform may require movement and resettlement. The individual cultivator will have to assume responsibilities of ownership he did not have to exercise under systems of semi-feudal tenure or communal landholding.

The loosening of traditional ties makes economic progress easier in certain respects. A man may work with a better will when he knows that the fruits of his labor will accrue to himself and his children instead of being dispersed among a number of dependents. Traditional communities are gov-

84

MEXICO. The child's greatest need after the age of six or seven is an education—an education that will enable him to play a useful role in the development of his community and country. (UNESCO photo)

UGANDA. The developing countries need every kind of educated person—administrators, doctors, teachers, engineers, literate workers, and farmers. Only the schools can provide them.

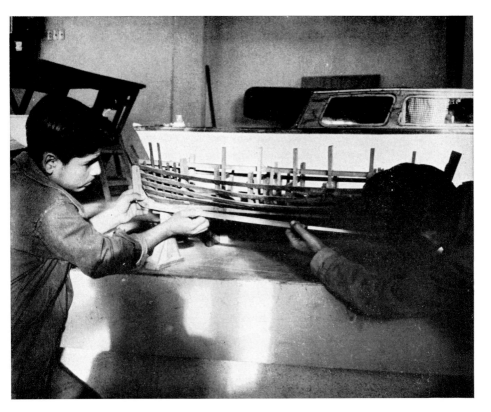

CHILE. There is now a widespread movement to give a more practical orientation to formal schooling, as in this Chilean fishing port.

KENYA. Vocational training and guidance are the final stages in the protective care due the rising generation. If these are well provided for, society will receive an immediate return on its investment. If not, both society and the individual will be losers.

INDIA. Change is the rule everywhere in the developing world today.

HONG KONG. A basic problem of this century is easing the transition
between rural and urban ways of life.

INDONESIA. In times of rapid change the adult can sometimes afford to wait a few years for things to improve, but the growing child cannot.

SIERRA LEONE. Village women's clubs are a prominent part of the community development movement in some countries. The specific task of the social services is to help families bridge the gap between old and emerging patterns of existence.

erned by the old folk who are deemed to be wise, experienced, and best acquainted with custom; rural improvements are easier to inaugurate if these village elders no longer exercise an unqualified veto over anything new.

But new village and agrarian institutions, adapted to the economic conditions that now prevail, have been slow to develop. Their growth is impeded by the cleavages forming between different social groups. The difference in outlook between the old and the young tends to be extreme. Equally great can be the gulf that develops between men and women of the same generation. Sometimes the man has been to school. Often, by venturing beyond his village and tribal confines, he has acquired a new outlook; whereas tradition itself, as if realizing that the woman is its last stronghold, has done all it could to keep her away from the modernizing influences of school and travel.

In the rural community dominated by rigorous traditions, the child may have had little opportunity to develop as an individual, but he was protected to the best of the community's ability, even if his parents sickened or died. As the strength of traditional institutions declines, some substitute means must be found to provide the child with the the security he requires. With good schooling and proper social guidance he may be in a position to mediate between traditional cultural patterns and the modern civilization with which he becomes acquainted at school. But even under the most favorable circumstances, he will have a different role, and in existing circumstances, often an impossible one.

SOCIAL CHANGE AND URBAN GROWTH

Large-scale urbanization appears to be one of the inevitable consequences of the economic and social trends of our era. A basic social problem of this century is easing the transition between rural and urban ways of life. In 1900 about 89 million persons, or 5.5 per cent of the world's population, lived in cities of 100,000 or more inhabitants. By 1950 their number had increased to 314 million, or 13.1 per cent of the world population; by 1960 (according to provisional estimates) to 448 million, or 14.9 per cent of the global population.

PERCENTAGE OF TOTAL POPULATION OF VARIOUS REGIONS LIVING IN CITIES OF 100,000 OR MORE INHABITANTS (Provisional 1960 estimates)	
Oceania	51%
North America	34%
Europe	23%
USSR	21%
Latin America	20%
Asia	10%
Africa	7%

This great cycle of urbanization started with the industrial revolution. In the economically advanced countries, though the end is still nowhere in sight, the rate of urban growth has somewhat slackened in the present century. In the developing countries, on the other hand, the rate of urban growth has been accelerating since 1900. Asia and Africa still lag in degree of urbanization because of their late start, but they are rapidly gaining. Between 1900 and 1960, it is estimated, the number of persons living in large cities increased from 1.4 million to 17.3 million in Africa; and from 19 million to 166 million in Asia. It is estimated that the population of the city of Leopoldville alone rose from about 119,000 in 1947 to about 400,000 in 1959, an increase of approximately 230 per cent in twelve years.

In Latin America massive urbanization is not so recent a phenomenon as in other parts of the developing world. This is traditionally a region of large capitals and sparsely settled hinterlands. But even here the tendency toward concentration in urban centers has been gathering momentum in the present century. If present rates of growth continue, the population of Latin America as a whole will double in 30 years, whereas the population of most of its large cities will double in under 18 years.

While the developing world (except for parts of Latin America where a "medium degree" of urbanization has already been attained) is still predominantly rural, the urban population of its various regions is currently increasing by 4½ to 5 per cent a year—about double the combined rural and urban rate of growth. Since higher rates of natural increase are found in rural areas than in the cities, it is evident that a large-scale migration to these urban centers is taking place. A recent UNESCO study* concluded that in a number of Latin American countries internal migration contributed half, and in some cases two-thirds, of the increase in the urban population in the 10 or 12 years preceding the censuses carried out around 1950.

In part, this migration to the cities is a healthy response to new opportunities in industry and trade, but to an even greater extent it appears to be a flight from rural poverty. It is a disturbing fact that in almost all the developing countries urban populations have increased much faster than new job opportunities. Hope more often than opportunity leads the villager to the metropolis.

In the urban environment—which means, for the great majority of the new arrivals from the countryside, a slum environment—the disintegration of social structures that has begun in rural areas often becomes precipitate. It may even extend to the breakdown of the basic family unit of parents and minor children.

Many men migrate alone to the cities, leaving their wives and children behind them. Perhaps they plan to return to their villages when they have

---

* *Urbanization in Latin America,* Edited by Philip M. Hauser, UNESCO, 1961.

made a stake, or to send for their families when they are comfortably established. For many, however, this is a day that never arrives. With only his unskilled labor to sell—and the exchange value of unskilled labor is extremely low in the developing countries—the new arrival is hard-pressed to obtain sufficient food for survival. Often the man is part of an unstable migrant labor force, drifting between city and country. He may set up a second household in the city—eventually to desert his original family if this new arrangement lasts, or to desert his city family if he returns permanently to the country.

The towns and cities also attract large numbers of young people seeking employment or anxious to escape the domination of traditional institutions. Lacking the skills and disciplines required for industrial employment, many of these youths fail to find steady work. Becoming increasingly discouraged and losing hope, they often drift into delinquency.

THE IMPACT ON MOTHERS AND CHILDREN

The mother and children left behind when the father goes to the city are faced with grave problems. The strain on the mother is severe, since upon her falls the main burden of adjusting the family to changing conditions and holding together what is left of it. In such circumstances, the task of bridging the hiatus between traditional and modern ways of life falls increasingly to the woman. Unfortunately, she seldom has the benefit of any formal education, and is ill-prepared for this task.

The mother and children who accompany the father to the city also face grave problems of adaptation. In a number of metropolitan regions, shanty-towns, make-shift shelters, and slums house as much as a third or even half the population. A good proportion of these are recent immigrants from the countryside. While conditions of housing and sanitation may be no worse than in many rural villages, the sheer size of the urban conglomeration and the promiscuous crush of urban humanity are factors with which the new arrivals are seldom prepared to deal.

In most cases the mother will find it impossible to feed her children with the money her husband can earn. She must look for work herself, and will have no one to care for her young children during her absence. Frequently the children roam the streets. Some drift completely away from their homes and become vagrants. Fending for themselves by odd jobs, such as shining shoes or selling papers, or exploited by unscrupulous employers, they become easy prey to every chance temptation, and may turn to begging, scavenging, or stealing. The juvenile street gang, practicing its own subsistence economy based on petty thievery, may be the only mutually protective group to which these children—or the youths who migrate to the city without their families—can turn.

In some countries the instability of family relationships has resulted in an increasing number of children born out of either legal or customary wedlock. The financial difficulties confronting the mother who must be the sole support of her children are great. In some, though by no means all, communities the social position of the unmarried mother may be extremely difficult. Some infants born out of wedlock are abandoned. Abandoned or not, their birth often goes unregistered, and later in life they may encounter difficulties because they lack a legal identity.

Social stresses are by no means confined to the new immigrants to city slums—nor, for that matter, to the developing countries. But in these countries the stresses tend to be more severe than elsewhere, for changes that took a number of generations in today's economically advanced areas are being compressed into a few decades or less. Among the 24 developing countries that participated in the recent UNICEF-sponsored preliminary survey of the needs of children, a common desire stood out in bold relief: to find measures to ease the difficult transition from traditional to new ways of life and in so doing to preserve the family, guide the parents toward adequate employment, and teach them the essentials of health, nutrition, child care, and home economics.

DEVELOPMENT OF FAMILY AND CHILD WELFARE PROGRAMS

Family and child welfare programs are usually classified among the social services. All services relating to health, nutrition, housing, social security, labor, etc. can legitimately be described as social services in the broad sense. As employed by the United Nations, the term is restricted to the various organized efforts carried out by government or voluntary agencies to promote a better mutual adjustment of individuals and their social—that is to say, their human—environment. But even as so defined, the social services include, not only efforts to help the individual adjust to society, but broader social action programs.

In the economically advanced countries, the traditional role of the social services—and one which they have performed with a considerable measure of success—has been to help disadvantaged groups or individuals. At the same time cooperative effort to achieve desirable social change has been an important feature of their work. In the developing countries, social services of a comprehensive nature are a basic requirement if balanced economic growth and social development are to be achieved. For in these countries it is not a disadvantaged minority, but the majority of families and individuals who need help in undertaking cooperative ventures to improve their social environment and in adapting themselves to emerging conditions.

By themselves the social services can hardly solve the problems created by rapid economic and social change. Broader measures, planned and executed on a national level, are clearly needed—nation-wide programs of rural community development to make better use of the human and material resources of the countryside, improve the standards of rural life, and thus lessen the economic pressures driving workers off the land; the creation of urban jobs in lines of work that will contribute to further economic development; the establishment of new urban communities with enough space, light, and air for healthy living.

Social service personnel can, and should, contribute to the planning and execution of such broad measures. At the same time, the social services have their own *raison d'être* in a developing country: to help families and communities bridge the gap between old ways of life and new patterns of existence in an orderly, constructive manner. Particularly valuable are services which concentrate on group work and community organization. Where children are concerned, the primary aims of the social services are:

● To preserve and strengthen the protection afforded the child by the basic unit of his social environment, the family.

● To provide special protection for the abandoned, neglected or maladjusted child.

● As part of broader, long-range objectives, to promote a better social environment for the child and adolescent, both in the city and rural areas.

In the field of social welfare, as in other fields related to the needs of children, timely measures of prevention are clearly preferable to later remedial ones. But the funds available for social services in the developing countries are very small, and the problems requiring immediate remedial action receive first attention. Often, therefore, it is most practicable to provide preventive social services for families and children through the administrative framework of programs in such fields as health, nutrition, education, vocational training and guidance, housing, and community development. If this is done, persons concerned with family and child welfare should see that there is maximum cooperation and coordination among the various services that may be involved.

UNITED NATIONS AND OTHER INTERNATIONAL ASSISTANCE

A number of developing countries have begun to extend their social services, though the possibilities of effective government action in this area are still not so widely recognized as they are in regard to health, education, and nutrition. Expert assistance and material aid for family and child welfare have been extended to the developing countries through both United Nations and bilateral channels. A number of voluntary agencies have also developed programs of international assistance in this field. Within the United Nations system, major responsibility for technical advice on the development of family and child welfare services rests with the Bureau of Social Affairs of the United Nations Secretariat, which collaborates with UNICEF on its assistance program in this field.

Most of the developing countries still lack the basic legislative and institutional sub-structure that supports social services for children and other vulnerable groups in the economically advanced countries. The shortage of adequately trained personnel is a serious problem everywhere. Voluntary efforts usually account for a large proportion of existing services and constitute a valuable resource, but their coverage tends to be spotty, and difficult problems of coordination may arise. Thus far in international assistance, the greatest emphasis has been placed on training of staff, coordination of existing services, and the development of long-term comprehensive plans.

While the needs of the child in the rural environment do not differ basically from those of the child in a city environment, his social situation, and the measures that can best be taken to meet his needs may differ considerably. Rural community development and allied programs seem to be the most feasible approach to the special problems of rural families in an age of transition. Specialized social services seem to be more applicable to the urban scene, though, as the opportunity arises, they should be made available in some form and degree throughout the country. But even in the cities the traditional types of social services will not suffice. Experimentation with new methods is needed, particularly those related to town-planning, housing, and environmental sanitation efforts, neighborhood or district community development projects, and programs for the education of women and the vocational training of youth.

Rural community development programs—though not always so termed —feature prominently in the planning of a number of countries in Africa, Asia, the Eastern Mediterranean area, and the Americas. The value of successful community development projects in promoting the well-being of children cannot be overestimated. The object of community development is to fuse services available in such fields as health, welfare, nutrition, education, public works, and agricultural extension, into a coordinated effort in each rural locality and to stimulate popular initiative, self-help, and mutual aid among villagers.

Social service techniques—particularly for organizing group activities involving women and youth—can make an important contribution to com-

90

munity development. As part of the community development movement, some countries, notably in Africa, have encouraged and assisted the organization of village women's clubs. At these clubs, young women and mothers learn improved methods of child-rearing and are given practical instruction in hygiene, diet, and home economics. They learn by doing. This type of training is especially important for the girls and younger women who will have the task of keeping family life intact under changing economic and social conditions.

A number of the 42 family and child welfare projects that UNICEF was aiding by the end of 1962 were being carried out as part of a community development approach. Besides providing supplies to help these projects get into action, UNICEF grants stipends and other forms of aid for the training of all kinds of staff, from teachers, supervisors, and professional social service personnel down to village-level workers, local agency board members, and volunteers.

In Pakistan, the Government is extending the community development approach to seven major urban areas. Like the rural projects, the urban community development projects are based largely on the self-help principle. A survey of Karachi in the late 1950's revealed that about 120,000 families, accounting for a third of the metropolitan population, were without reasonable shelter, and that only 60 per cent of the children were in school. It also revealed extremely poor conditions of environmental sanitation and a paucity of adequate health services. The Government is taking important steps toward civic improvement, but is counting on the people themselves to provide local leadership and to carry out most of the necessary work. In all, some 25 separate community development areas have been mapped out in Pakistan's principal cities, each covering 40,000 persons.

A local council is in charge of the development effort in each of these areas and is responsible for requesting the particular type of aid it needs. The government assigns to each project area two trained community organizers, a man and a woman, who encourage, lead, and coordinate development efforts. The projects lay great emphasis on the health and welfare of mothers and children; they include women's centers, boys' and girls' clubs, and maternal and child health centers. Since 1959 the Government of Pakistan has budgeted more than $700,000 to urban community development and UNICEF has allocated $121,500 to support its efforts. International experts recruited by the United Nations Bureau of Social Affairs and assigned under the United Nations' Expanded Program of Technical Assistance have aided in planning and organizing the program.

The social services proper have entered more readily into the urban than into the rural picture in most countries. Traditionally, the social services were first organized to deal with urban child and family problems. Experience has shown that the type of professional leadership needed in the growing urban conglomerations of the developing countries is the kind social workers can provide. In Costa Rica, for example, UNICEF and the United Nations Bureau of Social Affairs are assisting the government in a program to train social workers and supervisors, administrative employees involved in mother and child welfare programs, and non-professional auxiliaries working directly with children in residential institutions and day-care centers. Six community centers are being established for demonstration and training.

The social services most urgently needed in the developing countries today are those designed to serve large groups faced by a wide diversity of problems. In both rural and urban areas, social service activities can frequently be planned and executed in the context of larger, multipurpose projects. Whether or not this particular approach is followed, it is important for social service programs to be closely coordinated with other development efforts; for in most communities, little progress can be made in social welfare without concurrent progress in health, nutrition, education, housing, and the like.

UNICEF is currently providing about $2 million a year to aid family and child welfare services. Primarily, UNICEF wishes to encourage programs designed to keep the family together and improve the care given children in their own homes. Aid is also available to raise the standards of care in orphanages and other institutions for homeless children, but governments are being encouraged to find better ways of providing for the child needing some kind of full-time care outside his own home—adoption, foster-family placement, or group homes, for example.

Day-care centers are being stressed as one of the most practical ways of helping the family meet its responsibilities to the child when both parents must work. Day care is a prominent feature of a number of UNICEF-aided programs in Asia, and may eventually take its place, along with public health and education, as an essential service in areas where it is rapidly becoming the accepted norm for the wife as well as the husband to work in a factory, shop, or other commercial establishment. Properly run day-care centers can do a great deal to improve standards of child care in poorer communities. They do not have to be confined to the cities. In Taiwan, for example, 106 day-care centers have been established, and 22 new ones are planned, for farmers' children whose mothers must spend their days working in the fields.

CHAPTER VI

UNICEF: Its Nature and Function

Uɴɪᴄᴇꜰ is the only branch of the United Nations devoted entirely to the welfare of children. Its specific mission is to encourage and assist the governments of the economically less developed countries in undertaking long-term measures to meet the outstanding needs of their children.

Children have special needs as young and growing individuals. They constitute the most vulnerable group of the population, the group most at the mercy of an adverse environment. About three-quarters of the world's children are growing up in countries where family poverty and privation are the rule rather than the exception. It is widely agreed that a much higher rate of economic growth must be attained in these countries if living conditions are to be significantly improved; priority is therefore usually given to measures aimed primarily at raising national levels of production and income.

It would be disastrous, however, if forward-looking people were to lose sight of the fact that economic development must be accompanied by social development and that the planned use of a country's present and potential human resources is as important as the development of its soil, its mines, and its industry. It would be particularly disastrous for them to lose sight of the fact that the child, though temporarily a charge to the economy rather than a productive asset, represents the nation's future.

In all countries there are people in government, in the professions, in private agencies, in volunteer groups, and in all walks of life who wish to bring about an improvement in the lot of children. The goal of ᴜɴɪᴄᴇꜰ is to encourage and stimulate their efforts by providing the kind of international help that can be used as a lever for mobilizing local resources on behalf of children. Uɴɪᴄᴇꜰ assists governments in planning to meet the needs of their children within the framework of their broader programs for economic and social development. Its support to specific projects in the fields of health, nutrition, education, and social welfare is designed to enable countries to undertake comprehensive programs for the benefit of children that they could not carry out without key international assistance.

HISTORY

UNICEF, originally known as the United Nations International Children's Emergency Fund, was established by the United Nations General Assembly in December 1946 to give relief to children, primarily in war-devastated countries. In its first three years, the Fund's resources were devoted to bringing emergency aid (mainly food, but also some clothing and medical supplies) to fourteen war-devastated countries in Europe and to China. It also provided emergency relief to Palestine refugee mothers and children from 1948 to 1952.

With recovery in Europe, the General Assembly in 1950 directed UNICEF to turn its attention from emergency aid to long-term programs to improve the health and nutrition of children in the economically underdeveloped countries. In 1953 the Assembly voted to make UNICEF a permanent activity of the United Nations. Its name was shortened to United Nations Children's Fund, but the initials "UNICEF" were retained since they had become a well-known symbol. A new field of UNICEF assistance was added in 1958—social services for children and their families.

A study, entitled *The Needs of Children*, was carried out in 1961 by UNICEF and the other United Nations agencies most directly concerned with the problems of children and youth. The study was based, in part, on reports from governments receiving UNICEF aid. It revealed a growing realization of the importance of preparing children and young people to contribute in later life to the development of their countries. Accordingly, UNICEF has now broadened the scope of its assistance so that countries may receive aid for programs directed toward all high-priority aspects of their children's development, including education. UNICEF is also prepared to help countries ascertain the main needs of their children, plan programs to meet these needs, and, wherever possible, integrate these programs into their larger social and economic development efforts.

ORGANIZATION

UNICEF is a part of the United Nations proper, but it has a semi-autonomous status. It is governed by a thirty-nation Executive Board, ten members being elected each year by the Economic and Social Council of the United Nations. The Executive Board meets twice a year to establish policy, consider requests, allocate aid, evaluate results, and determine the Fund's administrative budget. The Board decides what types of program are to receive UNICEF aid and the conditions under which UNICEF aid will be granted. The actual day-to-day operation of UNICEF is the responsibility of an Executive Director who is appointed by the Secretary-General of the United Nations in con-

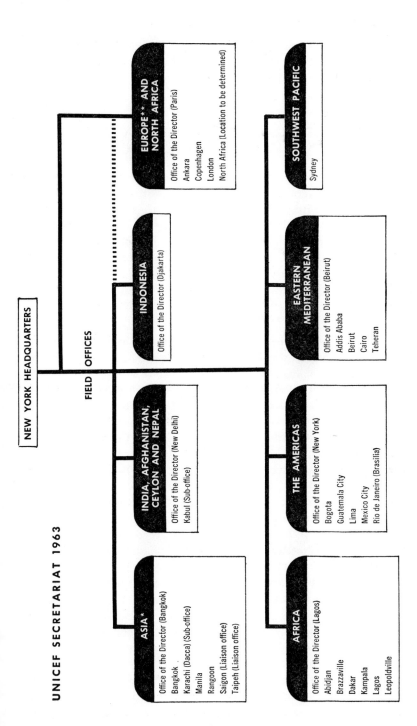

UNICEF SECRETARIAT 1963

NEW YORK HEADQUARTERS

FIELD OFFICES

ASIA*
Office of the Director (Bangkok)
Bangkok
Karachi (Dacca) (Sub-office)
Manila
Rangoon
Saigon (Liaison office)
Taipeh (Liaison office)

INDIA, AFGHANISTAN, CEYLON AND NEPAL
Office of the Director (New Delhi)
Kabul (Sub-office)

INDONESIA
Office of the Director (Djakarta)

EUROPE AND NORTH AFRICA**
Office of the Director (Paris)
Ankara
Copenhagen
London
North Africa (Location to be determined)

AFRICA
Office of the Director (Lagos)
Abidjan
Brazzaville
Dakar
Kampala
Lagos
Leopoldville

THE AMERICAS
Office of the Director (New York)
Bogota
Guatemala City
Lima
Mexico City
Rio de Janeiro (Brasilia)

EASTERN MEDITERRANEAN
Office of the Director (Beirut)
Addis Ababa
Beirut
Cairo
Teheran

SOUTHWEST PACIFIC
Sydney

*Excluding India, Afghanistan, Ceylon, Nepal, and Indonesia.

**Most of the work of this office is related to "Headquarters" functions — coordination with specialized agencies, public information, procurement, etc. — but it also directs some field work.

sultation with the Executive Board. The UNICEF Secretariat is a staff of approximately 590 persons located at the United Nations headquarters in New York and in some 30 regional, area, and country offices throughout the world.

RELATION TO GENERAL ASSEMBLY
AND ECONOMIC AND SOCIAL COUNCIL

UNICEF operates within the framework of resolutions adopted by the General Assembly of the United Nations and in accordance with such principles as may be established by the Economic and Social Council. Its work is reviewed annually by the Council and the Assembly. The Assembly and the Council have directed that UNICEF's resources must be used primarily to aid programs of long-range value in the economically less developed countries and that its operations must be effectively coordinated with the technical assistance programs of the United Nations and the Specialized Agencies.

COOPERATION WITHIN THE UNITED NATIONS

Administration of UNICEF-aided projects is the responsibility of the governments of the countries, which provide buildings, labor, and locally available supplies. International technical assistance is provided by the appropriate technical agencies of the United Nations system. Many of the international experts who work on UNICEF-aided projects are sent out under the Expanded Program of Technical Assistance. In the past, UNICEF has had its closest relations with the Food and Agriculture Organization (FAO), the World Health Organization (WHO), and the United Nations Bureau of Social Affairs. Now, as the scope of its assistance widens, UNICEF is being brought into close relation with the International Labour Organisation (ILO) and the United Nations Educational, Scientific and Cultural Organization (UNESCO). Through the cooperative use of their resources, UNICEF and the technical agencies can render effective assistance that none of them could offer alone. Thus, duplication and fragmentation of efforts are avoided.

Day-to-day cooperation between UNICEF and the technical agencies is extremely flexible. Both at headquarters and in the field, UNICEF and agency staff members confer and work together informally as the need arises. Two of the agencies, WHO and FAO, assign full-time advisors to work with the UNICEF headquarters staff. At a more formal level, representatives of UNICEF and each of the cooperating agencies attend the governing body meetings of the others. The UNICEF and WHO Executive Boards have established a joint health policy committee; similarly the UNICEF Executive Board and the FAO Council have established a joint policy committee. Scientific support for the campaign against protein malnutrition in children is provided by the joint

FAO/WHO/UNICEF Protein Advisory Group, composed of leading international authorities in this field.

In their cooperative programs, the division of responsibility between UNICEF and the technical agencies has been worked out as follows:

> Both UNICEF and the agencies assist governments in planning programs to meet the needs of their children, and both assist the government ministries concerned in drawing up concrete project plans of operations.
>
> UNICEF provides a variety of direct project assistance. It furnishes critical supplies and technical equipment—drugs, insecticides, clinic equipment, dairy plant equipment, vehicles, well-digging rigs, tools, teaching aids, etc.—seeing to the procurement and shipping of these, as well as paying for them. It provides direct financial support to training programs and training centers; in some cases, funds may be granted to provide stipends for students and to pay teachers' or professors' salaries. UNICEF also sends a certain number of skilled engineers into the field to assist governments in dairy plant and other food conservation projects.
>
> The technical agencies provide expert advice to UNICEF and to the governments. The UNICEF Executive Board does not approve aid for a particular project until the project plans of operation have received the technical approval of the agency or agencies competent in that field. In many instances, the agencies furnish experts to the governments for a few years to help them carry out approved projects. These arrangements ensure sound technical support for UNICEF-aided programs. Much of the aid given by UNICEF would not be practicable without the broader preparatory work that the technical agencies have carried out in their specialized fields.

UNICEF and the United Nations technical agencies also coordinate their activities, so far as possible, with bilateral aid given by various governments or groups of governments for programs directly or indirectly affecting children.

ESTABLISHING PROGRAM PRIORITIES

Not only are the unfulfilled needs of the world's children great and the means available to deal with these needs inadequate, but conditions vary widely from country to country and from region to region. Thus a partial strategy for attacking even the most critical of these needs cannot be dictated on a global basis or by any international body. UNICEF's policy is to adapt its aid to the special requirements of each country and its people, as de-

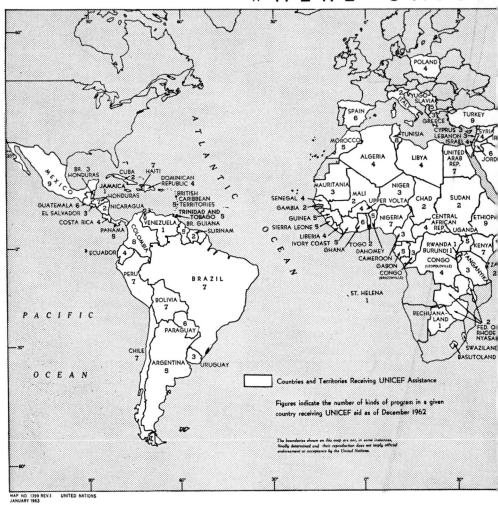

Countries and Territories Receiving UNICEF Assistance

Figures indicate the number of kinds of program in a given country receiving UNICEF aid as of December 1962

The boundaries shown on this map are not, in some instances, finally determined and their reproduction does not imply official endorsement or acceptance by the United Nations.

MAP NO. 1399 REV.1   UNITED NATIONS
JANUARY 1963

98

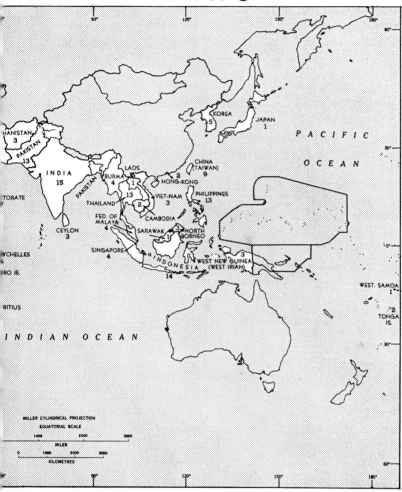

termined by the country itself, and to help each country in a way that builds on the services and facilities already existing.

The priorities a country assigns to the different programs of action that might be undertaken to meet the needs of its children should reflect, not only the relative importance of the different needs as such, but also the opportunities existing for effective action, the resources available, the technical feasibility of particular measures that might be employed, and the strategic importance various programs might have in relation to one another and as parts of a coherent plan. The last of these considerations is an important one. The soundest way to arrive at action priorities is through long-range planning based on an analysis of the outstanding needs of a country's children, once these needs have been determined by careful study of existing information, supplemented, where necessary, by field surveys.

While the establishment of action priorities in this manner is a matter for each government to undertake for itself, with international help if needed, certain conclusions that UNICEF has reached as a result of its experience with various types of project can prove valuable to governments wishing to take advantage of the international assistance available. International assistance benefits the greatest number of children if it is devoted to projects stressing preventive rather than curative or relief services. The long-range impact of this assistance can be multiplied by favoring projects of a seminal character; that is, projects that encourage the active participation of the populace concerned and have a broad educational value, that stress the training of badly needed skilled personnel, and that establish organizational patterns which could be extended to, or duplicated in, other parts of the country.

Since a child's welfare depends ultimately on conditions in his community, the best results can be expected if a number of environmental problems are attacked simultaneously, and if measures for children are fitted into broader measures to improve family and community living conditions in general. Hence UNICEF encourages multi-purpose programs involving the widest possible use of available organization resources. To avoid fragmentation of effort, UNICEF particularly urges governments, wherever possible, to integrate new programs for children into the pattern of existing services.

MATCHING UNICEF ASSISTANCE FROM LOCAL RESOURCES

UNICEF operates no field projects of its own. The projects it assists are primarily the responsibility of the governments which administer them. Most of the resources necessary to carry out these projects are provided by the governments concerned; these are known in United Nations terminology as "matching funds." Indeed, the governments are normally expected to provide for all local costs (though this requirement may be partially waived under certain circumstances), and one of the criteria UNICEF uses in passing on assistance requests is whether or not a given project appears to be one that a country can afford to carry out. Matching is not an end in itself; its purpose is to ensure a project's being firmly rooted in the country as a basic responsibility of the government.

In recent years, governments have provided on the average an equivalent of $2.50 in matching funds for every $1.00 allocated by UNICEF. These figures considerably understate the contribution of the countries since they do not include the cost of non-governmental efforts and contributions, or the expenses of continuing the program after UNICEF help has ceased.

OTHER CONDITIONS RELATING TO AID

In order for a government to receive aid, UNICEF and each receiving government conclude an agreement providing:

- That the government shall maintain accounting and statistical records on the receipt and distribution of UNICEF supplies, and furnish UNICEF with such records, reports, and information as may be necessary.

- That UNICEF officers be permitted to observe the handling, distribution, and use of supplies and equipment furnished by the Fund, and have access to accounts and other records of supplies received and distributed.

- That supplies provided by UNICEF are to be used or distributed equitably and efficiently on the basis of need, without discrimination because of race, creed, nationality status, or political belief.

- The UNICEF may at its discretion place distinctive markings on supplies provided by it in order to show that the supplies are provided under its auspices.

- That the receiving government shall cooperate with UNICEF in making available to the public adequate information concerning UNICEF assistance.

DEVELOPMENT OF A REQUEST FOR AID

Aid for a project is given only in response to a government request. A major function of UNICEF's field staff is to help governments plan the most effective use of the resources UNICEF can provide. If the request appears well founded, a draft "plan of operations" for the proposed project is worked out in discussion among the government departments, the staff members of UNICEF, and staff members of relevant technical agencies. The plan sets out in detail the objectives of the project; the plan of action; the administrative organization; and financial and other commitments to be undertaken by the government; the commitments to be undertaken by UNICEF; commitments of the technical agencies involved; and a target time schedule for carrying the project through its various phases.

If the plan receives technical agency approval and is recommended by the Executive Director of UNICEF as conforming to the assistance policies and financial capacities of the Fund, it is then examined by the fifteen-nation Program Committee of the UNICEF Board. On the basis of the Program Committee's recommendation, the proposal is then submitted to the Executive Board for allocation of funds.

To encourage long-term government planning and commitment, the Board may, at the time of its initial consideration, approve its support to a project for a period of several years. This approval is a formal commitment on the part of the Board to give the project priority for allocations up to the total amount of UNICEF aid envisaged in the plan of operations. Funds are usually allocated for the next twelve months only.

PROJECT IMPLEMENTATION

With the approval of aid by the UNICEF Board the stage of project implementation begins. The draft plan of operations is transformed into an agreement among the government, UNICEF, and the technical agencies concerned. The government takes steps to ensure the necessary administrative organization and financing, and the provision of supplies, facilities, and services to be provided locally.

UNICEF's work does not stop with the provision of supplies. The UNICEF field staff maintains continuous liaison with the project through each stage of implementation. The relevant agencies provide technical advice, and help the ministry administering the project to evaluate progress. In some instances they also provide experts to work on the projects for specified periods of time.

HOW UNICEF IS FINANCED

ANNUAL INCOME

UNICEF receives an annual income from voluntary government contributions, private contributions, and such other sources as the sale of greeting cards and interest on bank deposits.

CONTRIBUTIONS FROM GOVERNMENTS

Annual contributions to UNICEF from governments averaged approximately $22.7 million a year for the period 1960-2. This compares with an average of $11.9 million annually from governments for the period 1951-4.

The number of governments contributing in 1951 was 35. By 1954 the number had reached 61, and in 1962, 104. The size of each government contribution to UNICEF is decided by the individual government and is not determined by any UNICEF formula or scale of assessment.

The table on pages 104 and 105 shows government contributions to UNICEF for the years 1960-2. The sixteen largest contributors—those contributing an average of $200,000 or more a year during the period 1960-2— are listed below in order of the magnitude of their contribution:

United States of America	Mexico
Germany, Fed. Rep. of	Sweden
France	Switzerland
United Kingdom	Brazil
Canada	Iran
Union of Soviet Socialist Republics	New Zealand
India	Philippines
Australia	Yugoslavia

REVIEW OF 1962 CONTRIBUTIONS

The United States is the largest contributor. Its pledge was $12 million for 1962. The United States has for some years declared that its contributions should represent a decreasing percentage of the total. The financial support of other governments increased from $10.9 million for 1961 to $11.5 million for 1962. The Federal Republic of Germany contributed $1,375,000; France contributed $1,109,000. The USSR, Byelorussia and the Ukraine together contributed $862,500. Canada raised its contribution to $740,741, and Sweden raised its contribution to $500,000. Other governments announced increased pledges in the course of 1962.

UNICEF's resources must continue to grow as they have in the past if it is to meet the increasing number of requests it is receiving for strategic aid in carrying out soundly planned programs for children.

OTHER SOURCES OF INCOME

UNICEF income from private sources comes mainly from educational projects such as the Hallowe'en programs in the United States and Canada, "milk-days" in some European countries, and the proceeds of the world-wide sale of greeting cards. Churches and women's groups, schools, and individuals also make contributions. Private contributions rose from $2.7 million in 1961 to $3.2 million in 1962. Net income from greeting card sales rose from $900,000 in 1960 to $1.1 million in 1962. In Australia and New Zealand, the

103

COUNTRY	1960	1961	1962
Afghanistan	$ 10,000	$ 10,000	$ 10,000
Argentina	18,072	60,241	45,455
Australia	537,600	537,600	537,600
Austria	47,231	46,154	57,919
Belgium	160,000	160,000	160,000
Brazil	478,000	307,787	287,375
British Caribbean Territories:			
Antigua	117	116	117
Bahamas	—	2,800	—
Barbados	—	756	—
Grenada	583	—	1,167
St. Lucia	—	—	1,744
British Honduras	350	350	349
Brunei	1,633	3,267	3,267
Bulgaria	7,353	7,353	4,274
Burma	56,000	56,000	56,000
Byelorussian Soviet Socialist Republic	37,500	62,500	62,500
Cambodia	3,000	3,500	3,000
Cameroun	—	8,163	8,163
Canada	670,751	630,177	740,741
Central African Republic	—	3,811	2,861
Ceylon	14,726	14,726	14,726
Chad	—	8,065	—
Chile	80,000	80,000	80,000
China	15,000	15,000	15,000
Colombia	11,429	159,804	150,000
Congo (Brazzaville)	3,930	7,560	7,734
Congo (Leopoldville)	—	—	17,000
Costa Rica	30,000	30,000	30,000
Cuba	75,659	70,000	70,000
Cyprus	—	—	1,000
Czechoslovakia	34,722	34,722	52,083
Dahomey	5,000	—	5,000
Denmark	72,400	144,800	173,760
Dominican Republic	20,000	—	20,000
Ecuador	10,000	10,000	10,000
El Salvador	20,000	20,000	20,000
Ethiopia	18,000	18,000	18,000
Finland	19,688	50,937	50,938
France	748,240	1,109,184	1,109,184
Gabon	5,000	102	10,204
Gambia	1,680	560	560
Germany, Federal Republic of	595,238	1,375,000	1,375,000
Ghana	16,800	16,800	16,800
Greece	32,000	32,000	57,000
Guatemala	—	20,000	30,000
Guinea	8,097	—	—
Holy See	1,000	1,000	1,000
Honduras	20,000	20,000	—
Hong Kong	3,500	3,500	3,500
Hungary	12,876	12,876	12,876
Iceland	10,646	9,408	10,651
India	629,781	629,781	629,781
Indonesia	100,000	100,000	100,000
Iran	260,000	265,000	270,000
Iraq	56,000	28,058	41,943
Ireland	2,800	7,000	10,000
Israel	28,000	28,000	35,000
Italy	288,000	—	—

GOVERNMENT CONTRIBUTIONS TO UNICEF (Cont'd.)

COUNTRY	1960	1961	1962
Ivory Coast	—	—	10,204
Jamaica	8,396	8,385	8,385
Japan	150,000	150,000	170,000
Jordan	2,797	2,797	2,797
Kenya	—	—	280
Korea, Republic of	2,000	3,500	3,500
Kuwait	—	—	5,000
Laos	500	—	—
Lebanon	9,221	9,534	12,993
Liberia	5,000	5,000	—
Libya	7,000	4,500	4,500
Liechtenstein	702	930	1,000
Luxembourg	5,000	6,000	6,000
Madagascar	—	5,102	5,102
Malaya, Federation of	24,500	24,500	24,500
Mali	—	5,000	5,000
Mexico	500,000	500,293	500,000
Monaco	2,041	2,041	2,041
Morocco	17,921	20,000	25,000
Netherlands	78,947	82,873	82,873
New Zealand	210,000	210,000	210,000
Nicaragua	10,000	10,000	10,000
Niger	2,041	—	4,082
Nigeria	21,000	—	42,000
North Borneo	327	328	3,267
Norway	67,200	108,920	136,500
Pakistan	96,600	96,600	96,534
Panama	10,000	10,000	10,000
Paraguay	10,000	10,000	—
Peru	58,077	59,591	89,720
Philippines	125,000	125,000	205,000
Poland	50,125	60,000	60,150
Romania	25,000	25,000	—
Sarawak	8,167	8,167	8,167
Saudi Arabia	—	—	10,000
Sierra Leone	280	280	280
Singapore	6,533	6,534	6,533
Somalia	—	3,000	—
South Africa, Republic of	23,000	30,040	30,084
Spain	33,333	33,333	66,667
Sudan	9,969	9,978	10,000
Sweden	260,618	347,490	500,000
Switzerland	269,100	348,837	348,837
Syria	9,722	11,286	11,204
Thailand	78,576	123,326	139,111
Togo	—	—	4,500
Trinidad and Tobago	7,000	7,000	7,000
Tunisia	8,160	9,460	11,346
Turkey	194,444	194,444	194,444
Uganda	—	2,800	—
Ukrainian Soviet Socialist Republic	75,000	125,000	125,000
Union of Soviet Socialist Republics	500,000	675,000	675,000
United Arab Republic	106,908	106,908	94,710
United Kingdom	938,000	938,000	938,000
United States of America	12,000,000	12,000,000	12,000,000
Upper Volta	3,061	3,061	3,061
Viet-Nam, Republic of	7,500	7,500	7,500
Yugoslavia	200,000	200,000	200,000
	$21,517,168	$22,959,796	$23,559,144

SUMMARY OF ALLOCATIONS APPROVED BY THE EXECUTIVE BOARD FOR THE CALENDAR YEAR 1962 (in US dollars)

Program	Africa	Asia	East Med.	Europe	The Americas	Inter-Regional	Total	Per cent
HEALTH SERVICES	2,594,822	6,510,973	1,035,654	65,000	3,567,000	400,000	13,173,447	34.00
DISEASE CONTROL	685,088	3,845,807	1,961,503	19,000	4,360,000	—	10,871,398	28.12
Malaria eradication incl. DDT production	88	663,700	1,535,000	—	4,088,000	—	6,286,788	16.26
TB/BCG	93,000	1,538,500	252,003	19,000	272,000	—	2,174,503	5.62
Yaws/VD control	91,000	71,000	14,500	—	—	—	176,500	0.46
Trachoma control	30,000	949,607	91,000	—	—	—	1,070,607	2.77
Leprosy control	471,000	183,000	—	—	—	—	654,000	1.69
Other disease controls[a]	—	440,000	69,000	—	—	—	509,000	1.32
NUTRITION	1,516,000	4,120,590	56,000	325,000	931,893	1,750,561	8,700,044	22.50
Child feeding	—	257,590	—	—	631	850,000	1,108,221	2.87
Applied nutrition	1,516,000	1,863,000	56,000	61,000	852,000	683,561	5,031,561	13.01
Milk conservation	—	2,000,000	—	264,000	79,262	67,000	2,410,262	6.23
High-protein food development	—	—	—	—	—	150,000	150,000	0.38
FAMILY AND CHILD WELFARE	774,000	302,500	236,000	—	266,500	—	1,579,000	4.08
EDUCATION	467,400	652,000	460,000	268,000	608,000	—	2,455,400	6.35
VOCATIONAL TRAINING	276,000	—	—	—	225,000	—	501,000	1.30
COUNTRY PLANNING AND PROGRAM DEVELOPMENT	—	—	—	—	—	150,000	150,000	0.39
TRAINING SURVEY	—	—	—	—	—	2,433	2,433	0.39
TOTAL FOR LONG-RANGE AID	5,313,310	15,431,868	3,749,157	677,000	9,958,393	2,302,994	37,432,722	96.82
EMERGENCY AID	—	—	—	—	—	—	1,228,135	3.18
GRAND TOTAL FOR PROGRAM AID							38,650,857	100.00

Estimated operational services	} (last six months of 1962)	1,787,200
Estimated administrative costs		1,173,750
Estimated operational services	} (first six months of 1963)	1,858,400
Estimated administrative costs		1,148,375
GRAND TOTAL		44,628,582[b]

[a] Includes mycosis control $69,000 and penicillin production $440,000.

[b] The portion of the total approved allocations exceeding available resources in 1962, approximately $13.3 million (E/ICEF/P/L.292 para.12), will be entered in the UNICEF accounts effective 1 January 1963.

current Freedom From Hunger Campaign is being conducted as a joint UNICEF/FAO venture, the proceeds to be divided equally between the two agencies.

ALLOCATIONS, 1962

Program allocations by the UNICEF Executive Board totalled $44.6 million in 1962. In addition, it committed itself to future support for approved longer-term projects (principally in the field of nutrition) to the extent of $5.4 millions.

Over the next few years allocations to permanent health services, nutrition, social services, and education are expected to increase; aid to mass disease control campaigns is expected to remain at about its present level of $12 million a year, so that it will account for a progressively smaller percentage of the total.

EXPENDITURES

Expenditures (i.e., payment by UNICEF for supplies or services to fulfil allocations) may be spread over 6 to 12 or more months after allocations are made. Bids go out in the months following the Board session; but payments are made only when supplies are ready for shipment, which is often 6 months later, and longer in the case of special equipment. Some expenditures are not required until the latter part of the period for which an allocation is made. Delays in project operations may hold up provision of supplies by UNICEF. On any date, therefore, there are sizable allocations approved by the Board but not yet spent.

The unspent balance of allocations, plus any unallocated funds, constitute the "principal" of the Fund as referred to in the annual financial reports of UNICEF. Except for receivables (which consist mainly of government contributions pledged but not yet paid), the assets of UNICEF not needed for current supply or administrative commitments are invested in government securities of short and medium terms. Investment income accrues to the resources of the Fund. (The statement of UNICEF income and expenditures in 1961, as certified by the United Nations Board of External Auditors, is reproduced on page 108.)

OPERATIONAL SERVICES AND ADMINISTRATIVE COSTS

For the year 1963, the Board approved a budget of $3.7 million to cover operational services and $2.3 million to cover administrative costs. The costs budgeted to operational services include (a) the costs of the UNICEF field offices, since these field offices directly assist governments in the planning and implementation of projects, and (b) procurement and ship-

STATEMENT OF INCOME AND EXPENDITURE FOR THE YEAR ENDED
31 DECEMBER 1961

INCOME

    Contributions from governments

        (including receivables) $22,959,796.37

    Private contributions

        (including organized campaigns) 2,670,005.54

    Income from investments 972,215.08

    Staff assessment plan 318,618.07

    Agency procurement commission 75,000.00

    Miscellaneous income 1,031,262.82

                                       28,026,897.88

    Less: Difference in exchange 81,917.79 $27,944,980.09

EXPENDITURE

    Supplies and equipment 18,619,322.22

    Fellowships 561,404.09

    Project personnel 336,477.46

    Other non-supply assistance 441,814.88

    Operational services 2,507,780.24

                                         22,466,798.89

    Administrative costs 1,983,017.21   24,449,816.10

EXCESS OF INCOME OVER EXPENDITURE .... $ 3,495,163.99

CERTIFIED CORRECT: APPROVED:

(*Signed*) Stanley SROKA   (*Signed*) Maurice PATE

Comptroller   *Executive Director*

AUDIT CERTIFICATE

    The above statement of income and expenditure has been examined in accordance with our directions. We have obtained all the information and explanations that we have required, and we certify, as a result of the audit, that, in our opinion, the above statement is correct.

(*Signed*) L. GOTZEN, *Netherlands*

J. M. MURGUEITIO, *Colombia*

Ghulam ABBAS, *Pakistan*

ping costs (exclusive of freight which is covered by project allocations). Administrative costs include the salaries of headquarters and regional office personnel and headquarters and regional office expenses. The fact that the United Nations provides office space for UNICEF at headquarters and furnishes UNICEF a number of essential departmental services helps to minimize administrative expenditures, which in 1961 accounted for 8.1 per cent of the Fund's total expenditures.

For administrative and operational services in 1963, the UNICEF budget and country office local budgets provide for 625 posts—160 at UNICEF headquarters in New York and 465 for some thirty-one field offices. A total of 178 of these posts are internationally recruited; 447 are locally recruited.

The Executive Board has a Committee on Administrative Budget which examines in detail the annual administrative and operational services budget estimates of the Executive Director and makes recommendations concerning them to the Executive Board. The Committee also reviews the annual financial reports of UNICEF.

COOPERATION WITH VOLUNTARY ORGANIZATIONS, FOUNDATIONS, AND PRIVATE INDUSTRY

"Il faut entr'aider: c'est la loi de nature."
— La Fontaine

Many of the programs adopted under the United Nations system to establish better international relations and to improve social and health conditions in the developing countries were first conceived and promoted by private citizens working together in voluntary associations. Today there are approximately two thousand international associations of a private nature. In United Nations language these are known as non-governmental organizations. More of these are classified under "welfare, education, and youth" than under any other designation.

By promoting new ideas and developing new techniques and systems, non-governmental organizations working in the field of child welfare have frequently broken the ground for later governmental and international action. In many countries, voluntary organizations pioneered in developing maternal and child health and social welfare services. For example, religious missions have long been leaders in the rehabilitation of patients suffering from leprosy. Mission hospitals in some parts of the world still provide the nucleus of basic rural health services. The first declaration of the rights of the child was drawn up by a non-governmental organization, the International Union for Child Welfare, in 1923, and helped pave the way for the official Declaration of the Rights of the Child adopted by the United Nations General Assembly in 1959.

Seventy international non-governmental organizations (having more than three thousand national affiliates) have consultative status with the UNICEF Executive Board. These organizations help build communications between their constituents and other peoples throughout the world, and do much to develop a greater public awareness of the needs of the world's children. Furthermore, many of them conduct active field programs. In the developing countries the work of the voluntary organizations and that of UNICEF complement one another in many respects.

UNICEF's assistance is provided to governments for programs undertaken under government aegis and responsibility. While international voluntary organizations sometimes provide direct assistance to governments for specific child welfare programs, they usually work through affiliated national and local organizations. Volunteer personnel, some from non-governmental organizations, have worked on UNICEF-assisted projects in trachoma control, nutrition education, midwife training, and community development.

Non-governmental organizations have officially participated in a number of UNICEF-aided projects: for example, community development work in Uganda, the strengthening of social services in Guatemala, maternal and child health work in Pakistan, the rehabilitation of crippled children in Thailand. In addition, voluntary organizations have often been able to assist children's projects that did not, at the time, qualify for UNICEF or other United Nations aid. The experience these organizations have gained in meeting children's needs has been valuable to UNICEF in planning its own assistance.

Representatives of the seventy non-governmental organizations having consultative status attend the meetings of the UNICEF Executive Board. When some matter with which they are particularly concerned is under discussion, they submit reports for the Board's consideration. Both at headquarters and in the field, informal consultations between non-governmental organization representatives and UNICEF staff members are frequent, and close liaison is maintained on matters of mutual interest.

Many private institutions and industrial enterprises contribute in various ways to improve the condition of children, sometimes in association with UNICEF. Private foundations play a leading role in nutrition research. Industrial firms help establish and spread the technology for processing new foods. Foundations have assisted in the establishment of health services and in building and staffing schools; their assistance to governments in carrying out national surveys has been an invaluable contribution to sound project planning. The exchange of students and faculty members between universities in the more developed countries and those in the less developed countries has greatly facilitated the expansion of medical training, nutrition and health education, and agricultural extension work in the less developed areas.

110

Numerous business and commercial enterprises, industrial associations, and cooperatives, though not directly or indirectly associated with UNICEF in any official capacity, provide assistance to projects benefiting children, and frequently prepare the groundwork for larger-scale national or international assistance.

NATIONAL UNICEF COMMITTEES

In a score of countries national committees have been organized for UNICEF. These committees are generally composed of individuals and representatives of non-governmental organizations concerned about the needs of children in the less developed countries. The basic purposes of a UNICEF national committee are to stimulate interest on the part of the public and government in the needs of children; to provide the means for broad participation by private citizens in the work of UNICEF; and to accept contributions for UNICEF. These committees have been increasingly valuable in promoting a wider understanding of the problems of children and in gaining popular support for the work of the United Nations in helping governments to meet these problems.

Some national UNICEF committees conduct fund-raising and public information programs. Others join in special efforts, such as the FAO-sponsored five-year "Freedom From Hunger" campaign.

UNICEF GREETING CARDS

The UNICEF greeting card campaign began experimentally in 1949, when holiday designs were first offered to the public. Response was immediate, and by 1951 the greeting cards were established as an annual undertaking to stimulate public interest in the work of UNICEF. Each year designs are contributed by leading artists from various countries.

The greeting card project has now grown to the point where it serves to bring United Nations activity on behalf of children to the attention of millions of people all over the world every year, and also earns significant profits for child care aid. In 1960, over 17 million cards were sold, yielding a net profit of over $1 million. The continued growth in the sale of greeting cards is largely the result of interest and participation by national UNICEF committees, United Nations committees and associations, and many international and national non-governmental groups.

ANNEX

Selected Statistical Data

Table I^a

EXPECTATION OF LIFE AT BIRTH AND OF ADDITIONAL YEARS OF LIFE AT OTHER AGES

Country	Birth	5 years	15 years
AFRICA			
Congo (Léopoldville)			
African population	39	45	39
Guinea			
Rural population	31	40	35
Urban population	36	47	41
ASIA			
Ceylon	60	64	55
India	32	41	36
Japan	68	66	56
Philippines	51	59	51
Thailand	50	53	45
EASTERN MEDITERRANEAN			
United Arab Republic^b	38	54	46
EUROPE			
Federal Republic of Germany	69	67	51
France	71	68	58
Italy	67	67	57
Sweden	73	70	60
United Kingdom			
(England and Wales)	71	70	58
THE AMERICAS			
Brazil	42	48^c	41^c
Costa Rica	56	61	51
El Salvador	51	57	50
Guatemala	44	51	44
Mexico	39	50	43
Peru^b	46	52	45
United States	70	67	57

^a *Demographic Yearbook 1961* (United Nations publication sales No.: 62.XIII.1; pp. 622-641).

^b *Demographic Yearbook 1960* (United Nations publication sales No.: 61.XIII.1; pp. 602-609).

^c Men only.

Table II[a]
CALORIE AND PROTEIN CONTENT OF NATIONAL AVERAGE FOOD SUPPLIES
IN SELECTED COUNTRIES

Country	Period	Calories	Total Protein grams	Animal Protein grams
		. . . . per caput per day		
AFRICA				
Mauritius	1960	2350	45	11
Morocco[b]	1952–55	2350	72	18
ASIA				
Ceylon	1960	2150	47	9
India	1960–61	1990	53	6
Japan	1960	2240	68	18
Pakistan	1959–60	2080	48	7
Philippines	1960	1950	49	15
EASTERN MEDITERRANEAN				
Libya	1959	2180	53	10
Turkey	1959–60	2830	91	16
United Arab Republic	1958–59	2520	73	12
EUROPE				
Federal Republic of Germany	1960–61	2950	80	48
France	1959–60	2990	99	53
Italy	1960–61	2740	80	28
Sweden	1960–61	2920	81	53
United Kingdom	1960–61	3270	87	52
THE AMERICAS				
Brazil[b]	1958	2500	62	20
Chile[b]	1958	2450	78	27
Colombia	1956–58	2200	48	23
Ecuador	1957–59	2230	56	18
Mexico	1957–59	2440	68	20
Paraguay	1957–59	2500	68	26
United States	1960	3120	92	65

[a] *The State of Food and Agriculture 1962* (Rome: FAO, 1962; pp. 190-192).
[b] *The State of Food and Agriculture 1961* (Rome: FAO, 1961; pp. 169-171).

116

Table III
ESTIMATED GOVERNMENT EXPENDITURES IN TERMS
OF PERCENTAGE OF GROSS NATIONAL PRODUCT

Annual per caput income	All govt. expenditures	For economic purposes	For social purposes			
			Total	Education	Health	Other
Under $100						
India	15.8	6.3	2.3	1.4	0.6	0.3
Kenya	22.3	4.4	5.9	3.0	1.1	1.8
Tanganyika	14.0	4.0	4.3	2.7	1.2	0.4
Under $200						
Colombia	9.4	2.9	1.3	0.5	0.3	0.5
Ghana	17.7	6.7	5.0	2.5	1.1	1.4
Thailand	16.8	3.5	4.3	2.9	0.5	0.9
Under $500						
Chile	13.7	2.6	5.7	2.7	2.8	0.2
Federation of Malaya	20.1	3.5	5.5	3.5	1.5	0.5
Japan	21.1	9.2	6.3	1.5	0.5	4.3
Under $900						
Austria	23.5	6.3	9.3	2.5	0.1	6.7
Israel	39.5	14.9	12.8	3.9	2.2	6.7
Venezuela	18.7		3.2	1.2	1.2	0.8
Over $900						
Australia	27.0	7.2	11.3	2.0	2.1	7.2
United Kingdom	31.4	5.1	15.1	4.1	3.2	7.8
United States	30.4	4.2	9.4	3.8	1.1	4.5
Median	21.2	4.4	5.6	2.7	1.1	1.8

Source: *Report on the World Social Situation, 1961* (United Nations publication sales No.: 61.IV.4; p. 71).

TABLE IV

COUNT OF PROJECTS ASSISTED BY UNICEF AS OF DECEMBER 1962

NOTE: Each type of project in a particular country is counted only once, though there may be several separate projects of the same type in the country.

Type of project	PROJECTS CURRENTLY ASSISTED								PROJECTS PREVIOUSLY ASSISTED							TOTAL	
	Africa	Asia	East. Med.	Eur. ope	The Amer. icas	Inter-Re-gional	Total currently assisted Proj.	Total currently assisted Coun.	Africa	Asia	East. Med.	Eur. ope	The Amer. icas	Total previously assisted Proj.	Total previously assisted Coun.	Currently & previously assisted Proj.	Currently & previously assisted Coun.
HEALTH SERVICES	40	38	17	9	49	3	156	96	5	14	7	25	11	62	39	218	115
Basic MCH	32ª	18	14	3	21	3	91	85	2	5	2	4	5	18	18	109	102
Environmental sanitation	8	6	2	—	28ª	—	44	43	—	3	1	1	1	6	6	50	49
Handicapped children	—	5	—	4	—	—	9	9	—	2	2	7	—	11	11	20	20
Care of premature infants	—	1	1	2	—	—	3	3	—	—	2	7	1	10	10	13	13
Immunization	—	8	1	—	—	—	9	9	3	4	—	6	4	17	17	26	26
DISEASE CONTROL	45	48	27	4	38	—	162	88	21	27	24	38	32	142	86	304	116
Malaria	1	4ᵇ	6	—	23	—	34	34	12	4ᵇ	4ᶜ	6	—	26	26	60	60
Tuberculosis:																	
BCG vaccination	1	9	2	—	1ᵈ	—	13	13	5	10	12	10	19	56	53	69	65
Other	6	11	8	1	9	—	35	35	1	4	2	10	3	20	16	55	51
Treponemal disease																	
Yawsᵉ	13	7	—	—	—	—	20	20	3	6	—	—	7	16	16	36	36
Syphilis	1	1	1	1	—	—	4	4	—	1	1	8	—	10	9	14	13
Bejel/Syphilis	—	—	—	—	—	—	—	—	—	—	3	—	—	3	3	3	3
Leprosy	20	7	2	—	5	—	34	34	—	1	1	—	—	1	1	35	35
Trachoma	3	5	6	2	—	—	16	16	—	—	1	—	—	1	—	17	16
Typhus	—	1	—	—	—	—	1	1	—	1	—	—	2	3	3	4	4
Bilharziasis	—	1	1	—	—	—	2	2	—	—	—	—	—	—	—	2	2
Other diseases	—	2	1	—	—	—	3	3	—	—	1	4	1	6	4	9	7

NUTRITION	89	168	48	54	21	10	9	8	6	70	114	3	46	6	13	24	22
Maternal and child feeding	68	68	41	41	18	3	7	6	7	27	27	—	12	—	2	9	4
Applied nutrition	45	55	—	—	—	6	—	—	—	45	55	1	24[f]	2	6	6[f]	16[f]
Milk conservation	35	36	12	12	3	1	2	—	—	23	24	1	8	4	5	4	2
High-protein food development	4	5	1	1	—	1	—	—	—	3	4	1	1	—	—	2	—
Other nutrition projects[g]	3	4	—	—	—	—	—	—	—	3	4	—	1	—	—	3	—
FAMILY & CHILD WELFARE SERVICES	36	42	—	—	—	—	—	—	—	36	42	—	6	—	8	8	20[a]
Social services for children	27	27	—	—	—	—	—	—	—	27	27	—	6	—	7	7	7
Mothercraft and homecraft	12	12	—	—	—	—	—	—	—	12	12	—	—	—	1	—	12
Community development	3	3	—	—	—	—	—	—	—	3	3	—	—	—	1	1	1
EDUCATION	16	16	—	—	—	—	—	—	—	16	16	—	5	1	4	—	4
VOCATIONAL TRAINING	4	4	—	—	—	—	—	—	—	4	4	—	3	—	—	—	1
URBAN PROJECTS	1	1	—	—	—	—	—	—	—	1	1	—	1	—	—	—	—
EMERGENCY AID	44	46	39	40	6	14	5	10	5	6	6	—	—	—	3	1	2
GRAND TOTAL	137	799	21	298	70	87	45	57	39	116	501	6	148	20	72	121	134

[a] Including 1 area project.

[b] Includes 1 project for which UNICEF is providing only DDT production equipment.

[c] Includes 1 project for which DDT production equipment was also supplied.

[d] Includes 1 project for BCG vaccine production only.

[e] Some of these projects also provide treatment for syphilis.

[f] Including area projects in nutrition education and training.

[g] Goitre control and shark-liver oil encapsulation.

Table IV

AVERAGE YEARLY INCOME PER PERSON, 1957-1959
(For selected economically developed and developing countries)

Country	In US Dollars
United States	2100–2199
Australia	1100–1199
United Kingdom	900–999
Denmark	900–999
Mexico	200–299
Turkey	100–199
Brazil	100–199
Ghana	100–199
Guatemala	100–199
Iran	100–199
Burma	under 100
Ethiopia	under 100
Pakistan	under 100

Source: United Nations Statistical Office, July 1961.

Table VI
UNICEF EXPENDITURES ON MAJOR TYPES OF SUPPLIES AND SERVICES 1961*

(In thousands of US Dollars)

Transport: Vehicles	4,422.8
Advisory services: Fellowships, project personnel, other non-supply assistance	1,338.5
Equipment and supplies for health services:	
Basic equipment for health centers; training materials for nursing schools, hospitals, clinics; environmental sanitation and rehabilitation equipment; etc.	1,415.6
Drugs: Iron, calcium, and vitamin products; sulpha drugs; vermifuges; amebicides; scabicides; etc.	454.5
Vitamin A and D capsules	334.8
Soap	118.6
Equipment and supplies for disease control:	
Field laboratory equipment and supplies; sprayers and dusters; anti-malarials; TB X-ray units; BCG vaccines; antibiotic ointments; anti-leprotics; etc.	1,311.3
DDT	2,964.6
Dieldrin	299.1
Penicillin	128.1
Equipment and supplies for nutrition programs:	
Milk plant and food processing equipment	2,186.7
Foods, miscellaneous	353.2
Whole milk powder	349.3
Skim milk powder fortified with vitamins A and D	61.1
Supplies for emergency aid:	
Textiles and blankets	171.7
Miscellaneous supplies	345.6
	16,255.5
Freight:	
On powdered milk	2,030.4
On other supplies	1,641.0
Insurance reserve	32.1
TOTAL	19,959.0
*Note: In addition UNICEF spent $2,507.8 for operational services and 1,983.0 for administrative costs	4,490.8
Total expenditures	24,449.8

Table VII

SUPPLIES AND EQUIPMENT SHIPPED BY UNICEF

UNICEF makes purchases all over the world, wherever the best equipment and supplies can be obtained at the most advantageous prices. Generally government contributions are used to purchase supplies within the donor country for shipment abroad. Occasionally government contributions are used for overseas freight services.

ILLUSTRATIVE LIST OF SERVICES AND SUPPLIES SHIPPED FROM 1952 to 1962 SHOWING COUNTRY OF ORIGIN

Country of Origin	Type of Supplies
ARGENTINA	Vitamin capsules
AUSTRALIA	Bicycles, books, milk processing equipment, pharmaceuticals, poultry raising equipment, soap, tires and tubes, vitamin capsules, whole milk powder, wool
AUSTRIA	Medical supplies, microscopes and accessories, milk processing equipment
BELGIUM	Blankets, medical supplies and equipment, pharmaceuticals
BRAZIL	Overseas freight services
CANADA[1]	Books, cement, electric motors, environmental sanitation equipment, films, medical and laboratory equipment, publications, refrigerators, tires and tubes, vitamin capsules, whole and skim milk powder
CHINA	Sugar
COSTA RICA	Dried beans
CUBA	Sugar
CZECHOSLOVAKIA	Dental equipment, laboratory supplies, microscopes, motorcycles
DENMARK	BCG vaccine and supplies, medical and laboratory supplies and equipment, milk processing equipment, pharmaceuticals, whole milk powder
FINLAND	Pharmaceuticals
FRANCE	Anatomical models, antibiotics, BCG vaccine and supplies, books, charts, film projectors and films, garden tools, hardware, insecticides, medical and laboratory supplies, milk processing equipment, pharmaceuticals, soap, vehicles

[1] Canada has provided whole and skim milk powder from surplus stocks free of charge at shipside for shipment through UNICEF to country child welfare projects.

Table VII (Cont'd.)
ILLUSTRATIVE LIST OF SERVICES AND SUPPLIES SHIPPED FROM 1952 to 1962 SHOWING COUNTRY OF ORIGIN

Country of Origin	Type of Supplies
GERMANY, FEDERAL REPUBLIC OF	Baby scales, books, cement, diesel engines and generators, galvanized pipe, laboratory chemicals, medical and laboratory equipment, milk processing equipment, motor bicycles, orthopedic equipment, pharmaceuticals, stainless steel ware, surgical instruments, vehicles, vitamin capsules
GREECE	Dried fruits
ICELAND	Cod liver oil, dried cod fish
INDIA	BCG vaccine, gramophones
IRAQ	Dates
IRELAND	Fats, pharmaceuticals, whole milk powder
ISRAEL	Clothing, vehicles
ITALY	Medical supplies, microscopes, pharmaceuticals, sprayers and spare parts, vehicles, vitamin capsules
JAPAN	BCG vaccine, bicycles, blankets, cameras, cotton cloth, dental equipment, environmental sanitation equipment, fish oil encapsulating plant equipment, fishing nets, intravenous solution, microscopes, motor scooters, operating lights, refrigerators, sewing machines
LIECHTENSTEIN	Tires and tubes
MEXICO	BCG vaccine, books
NETHERLANDS	Insecticides, medical and laboratory supplies, milk processing equipment, pharmaceuticals, whole milk powder, X-ray equipment
NEW ZEALAND	Vitamin capsules, whole milk, wool
NORWAY	Laboratory equipment, margarine, pharmaceuticals, stainless steel ware, tires, vitamin capsules
PERU	Sugar
PHILIPPINES	BCG vaccine, coconut oil
POLAND	Midwife boxes, pharmaceuticals, sugar, surgical instruments
SPAIN	Blankets, scales, thermometers, tires and tubes

Table VII (Cont'd.)

ILLUSTRATIVE LIST OF SERVICES AND SUPPLIES SHIPPED FROM 1952 to 1962
SHOWING COUNTRY OF ORIGIN

Country of Origin	Type of Supplies
SWEDEN	Dental equipment, films, hospital supplies, laboratory supplies, milk processing equipment, office machines, stainless steel ware, X-ray equipment
SWITZERLAND	Hospital equipment, medical and laboratory supplies, milk processing equipment, pharmaceuticals, whole milk
THAILAND	BCG vaccine, rice
TURKEY	Beans, overseas freight services, rice, sugar
UNION OF SOVIET SOCIALIST REPUBLICS	Bicycles, blankets, cotton textiles, insecticides, sterilizers
UNITED ARAB REPUBLIC	BCG vaccine
UNITED KINGDOM	Antibiotics, bicycles and motorcycles, books and periodicals, environmental sanitation equipment, glassware, hospital supplies, laboratory chemicals, medical and laboratory supplies and equipment, milk processing equipment, pharmaceuticals, spare parts and tools, syringes, vehicles, X-ray and photographic equipment
UNITED STATES[1]	Antibiotics, BCG supplies, boats and outboard motors, books and journals, DDT and insecticides, dental equipment, diesel engines and spare parts, environmental sanitation equipment, films, fruit trees, galvanized pipe, garden tools, hospital supplies, laboratory chemicals, medical and laboratory supplies and equipment, milk processing equipment, orthopedic equipment, pharmaceuticals, playground equipment, poultry raising equipment, refrigerators, seeds, soaps, teaching materials, tires and tubes, vaccines and sera, vegetable seeds, vehicles and spare parts, well-drilling equipment, X-ray and photographic equipment
YUGOSLAVIA	Overseas freight services, pharmaceuticals

[1] Skim milk powder from surplus stocks was provided by the United States for shipment through UNICEF to country child welfare projects either at nominal cost (1952-54) or free of charge at shipside (beginning in 1955).

BIBLIOGRAPHY

CHAPTER I

1. *The United Nations Development Decade: Proposals for Action* (United Nations publication, Sales No.: 62.II.B.2).
2. *World Economic Survey 1961* (United Nations publication, Sales No.: 62.II.C.1).
3. *The Future Growth of World Population* (United Nations publication, Sales No.: 58.XIII.2).
4. Hoffman, Paul. *World Without Want* (New York: Harper & Brothers, 1962).
5. Hoffman, Paul. *One Hundred Countries: One and one-quarter billion people* (Washington, D. C.: Committee for International Economic Growth, 1960).
6. Hirshman, Albert. *The Strategy of Economic Development* (New Haven: Yale University Press, 1958).
7. Galbraith, John Kenneth. *Economic Development in Perspective* (Cambridge: Harvard University Press, 1962).
8. Schonfield, Andrew. *The Attack on World Poverty* (New York: Random House, 1960).

CHAPTER II

1. World Health Organization. *Planning of Public Health Services.* Report of the Expert Committee on Public Health Administration (*Wld Hlth Org. techn. Rep. Ser.* 215).
2. World Health Organization. *First Report on the World Health Situation,* 1954-56 (*Off. Rec., Wld Hlth Org.,* 94).
3. World Health Organization. *Second Report on the World Health Situation,* 1957-60 (in press).
4. World Health Organization. *The First Ten Years of the World Health Organization* (Wld Hlth Org., 1958).
5. World Health Organization. *Annual Epidemiological and Vital Statistics,* 1959 (Wld Hlth Org., 1962).
6. World Health Organization. *Deprivation of Maternal Care; A Reassessment of its Effects* (Wld Hlth Org., Public Health Paper 14).
7. World Health Organization. *Water Supply for Rural Areas and Small Communities* (*Monograph Series,* No. 42).
8. World Health Organization. *The Cost of Sickness and the Price of Health* (*Monograph Series,* No. 7).
9. World Health Organization. Expert Committee on Malaria. *Ninth Report* (*Wld Hlth Org. techn. Rep. Ser.* 234).
10. World Health Organization (1959), "Malaria eradication throughout the world" (*Chron. Wld Hlth Org.,* 13, 341).
11. World Health Organization (1961), "Origin and evolution of the treponematoses" (*Chron. Wld Hlth Org.,* 15, 226).
12. World Health Organization (1959), "Yaws: a disease in regression" (*Chron. Wld Hlth Org.,* 13, 208).
13. World Health Organization. Expert Committee on Trachoma. *Third Report* (*Wld Hlth Org. techn. Rep. Ser.* 234).
14. World Health Organization (1962), "Trachoma" (*Chron. Wld Hlth Org.,* 16, 364).
15. World Health Organization (1960), "International work in leprosy, 1948-1959" (*Chron. Wld Hlth Org.,* 14, 3-39).
16. World Health Organization. Expert Committee on Tuberculosis. *Seventh Report* (*Wld Hlth Org. Techn. Rep. Ser.* 195).
17. World Health Organization (1962), "Tuberculosis research" (*Chron. Wld Hlth Org.,* 16, 42).

18. World Health Organization (1959), "Nature and extent of the problem of bilharziasis" (*Chron. Wld Hlth Org.*, 13, 3-56).
19. World Health Organization. *The Role of Immunization in Communicable Disease Control* (Wld Hlth Org., Public Health Paper 8).
20. World Health Organization (1961), "Public Health Nursing" (*Chron. Wld Hlth Org.*, 15, 79-92).

CHAPTER III

1. Food and Agriculture Organization. *The State of Food and Agriculture, 1962* (Rome: FAO, 1962).
2. United States Department of Agriculture. *Food, The Yearbook of Agriculture, 1959* (Washington, D. C.: US Government Printing Office, 1959).
3. Galdstone, Iago, ed. *Human Nutrition, Historic and Scientific* (New York: International Universities Press, Inc., 1960).
4. *Humanity and Subsistence* (Geneva: Annales Nestlé, 1961).
5. McCormack, Arthur. *People, Space and Food* (London: Sheed and Ward, 1960).
6. Food and Agriculture Organization. *World Food Problems No. 1: Nutrition and Society* (Rome: FAO, 1956).
7. Food and Agriculture Organization. *World Food Problems No. 2: Man and Hunger* (Rome: FAO, 1957).
8. Burgess and Dean, eds. *Malnutrition and Food Habits* (New York: The Macmillan Company, 1962).
9. Waterlow, Cravioto, and Stephen. *Protein Malnutrition in Man* (New York: Academic Press, Inc., 1960).
10. Jelliffe, D. B. *Infant Nutrition in the Subtropics and Tropics* (Geneva: WHO, 1955).
11. Dean, R. F. A. *Treatment and Prevention of Kwashiorkor* (*Bull. Wld Hlth Org.*, 1953, 9, 767-784).
12. Food and Agriculture Organization. *Calorie Requirements* (Rome: FAO Nutritional Studies, No. 15, 1957).
13. Food and Agriculture Organization. *Protein Requirements* (Rome: FAO Nutritional Studies, No. 16, 1957).
14. *Protein Needs of Infants and Children* (Washington, D. C.: National Academy of Sciences — National Research Council, 1961).
15. World Health Organization (1960), "Endemic Goitre" (*Chron. Wld Hlth Org.*, 14, 337-365).
16. World Health Organization. *Milk Hygiene.* (*Monograph Series*, No. 48).
17. Kon, S. K. *Milk and Milk Products in Human Nutrition* (Rome: FAO Nutritional Studies, No. 17, 1959).
18. Food and Agriculture Organization. *Development through Food: a strategy for surplus utilization* (Rome: FAO, 1961).
19. Food and Agriculture Organization. *The Training of Auxiliary and Community Workers to Carry out Practical Nutrition Programs* (Rome: FAO, 1953).
20. United Nations Children's Fund. *Progress Report by the Executive Director on Results Achieved in FAO/WHO/UNICEF Protein-Rich Foods Program* (UNICEF Document E/ICEF/389, July 1959).

CHAPTER IV

1. *International Yearbook of Education* (Paris: UNESCO publication No. 224, 1960).
2. *World Survey of Education* (Paris: UNESCO vol. I, 1955; vol. II, 1958; vol. III, in press).
3. *Asia, Arab States, Africa: Education and Progress* (Paris: UNESCO, 1961).

4. *Final Report.* Conference of African States on the Development of Education in Africa (Paris: UNESCO/ED/181, 1961).
5. "Report on the regional meeting of representatives of Asian member states on primary and compulsory education" (Paris: UNESCO/C/PRG/3, 1960).
6. "Report on the educational needs of the Arab countries" (Paris: UNESCO/11/C/PRG/2, 1960).
7. "Report on the needs of Tropical Africa in the matter of primary, general secondary, and technical education" (Paris: UNESCO/11/C/PRG/1, 1960).
8. *Investment in Education.* The Report of the Commission on Post-School Certificate and Higher Education in Nigeria (Lagos, Nigeria: The Federal Government Printer, 1960).
9. Schulz, Theodore W. "Education and Economic Growth," *Social Forces Influencing American Education,* Nelson B. Henry, ed. (Chicago: University of Chicago Press, 1961).

CHAPTER V

1. *Report on the World Social Situation, 1957* (United Nations publication, Sales No.: 57.IV.3).
2. *Report on the World Social Situation, 1961* (United Nations publication, Sales No.: 61.IV.4).
3. *Urbanization in Asia and the Far East.* Philip M. Hauser, ed. (Paris: UNESCO, 1958).
4. *Urbanization in Latin America.* Philip M. Hauser, ed. (Paris: UNESCO, 1961).
5. *UNICEF-Aided Social Welfare Services Programs in Africa* (Leopoldville, Congo: Economic Commission for Africa, 1963).
6. "Day-Care Services for Children," *International Social Service Review* (United Nations publication, Sales No.: 55.IV.20).
7. *Social Aspects of Economic Development.* Economic Commission for Africa, Standing Committee on Social Welfare and Community Development (E/CN.14/SWCD/2, January 1962). Mimeographed.
8. Dulphy, G. "Problèmes sociaux et nutrition," *Nutrition et alimentation tropicales* (Rome: FAO, 1957; pp. 1771-1792).

INDEX

Abandoned children, 88

Agriculture, 8; backward practices of, 51; dependence on (chart), 50; extension programs, 61; modern techniques of, 56; relation to nutrition, 50-4

Alliance for Progress, 52

Allocations, 107; table of, 106

Amino acids, 65

Anemia, 49

Applied nutrition, UNICEF aid to, 62 ff.; in Bolivia, 63

Average yearly income per person (table), 120

Balanced economic and social development, 7 ff., 51

BCG, vaccination campaigns, 40; and Scandinavian welfare organizations, 40; WHO and UNICEF participation in, 40; vaccine, 39

Beri-beri, 49

Bilateral aid, 11-12

Bilharziasis, 20, 29, 41 ff.; UNICEF aid to control of, 42

Bureau of Social Affairs of the United Nations, 90, 91, 96

Calorie and protein content of national average food supplies (table), 116

Child, rights of, 5, 7

Children, abandoned, 88; handicapped, 26; health needs of, 19; illegitimate, 88; investment in, 9 ff.; needs of, 10; programs for, 1 ff.; spiritual needs of, 18

Chlor-tetra-cycline, 35

Clothing, 17

Colombo Plan, 12, 53

Commission on Post-School Certificate and Higher Education in Nigeria, Report of, 76

Commitments, 107

Communicable diseases, 20; campaigns against, 29 ff.; UNICEF aid to control of, 29; UNICEF policy of assistance to campaigns against, 42-3

Community development, 56-7, 89, 90

Conference of African States on Education, 5, 7, 74

Conjunctivitis, 35

Contributions, governments, to UNICEF, 102-5; table of, 104-5

Cottonseed flour, 68

Day-care centers, 5-6, 92

DDT, 31

Declaration of the Rights of the Child, 1, 18, 109

Deficiency diseases, goitre, 49, 63-4; protein, 45-6, 48; vitamin A, 10, 49; vitamin C, 49; vitamin D, 49

Developing countries, combined income of, 2; definition of, 2; poverty in, 3

Diamino-diphenyl-sulfone, 37

Diarrhea, 20, 24, 29, 50

Diseases of children, 19 ff., 29 ff.

Dysentery, 20, 50

Economic and Social Council, 8, 16, 94

Economic background of the developing countries, 2 ff.

Education, 71 ff.; in Brazil, 77-8; for life, 74; in health, 20, 25 ff.; in nutrition, 61-2; priorities of, 72-3; requirements for expansion of, 76-7; right to, 71; UNICEF assistance to, 77-8; United Nations assistance to, 77; of women, 90

Environmental sanitation, 20, 24 ff., 42, 90, 91; in urban slums, 87

Ethiopia, national nutrition program, 55

Expanded Program of Technical Assistance, 96

Expectation of life, 10; at birth (table), 115

Expenditures, 107

Eye diseases, 10, 20, 29, 35-6

Family and child welfare, 83 ff.; in Pakistan, 91; programs, development of, 80; UNICEF aid to, 91-2; United Nations assistance to, 89-90

Family planning, 4

Fish flour, 66; plant in Chile, 66

Food, 45 ff.; balance sheets, 49; consumption of (chart), 51; high-protein, 64-5; increased production of, 8, 52 ff.; production of and nutrition, 50-4

Food and Agriculture Organization of the United Nations (FAO), 45, 53, 55, 58, 96

Freedom from Hunger Campaign, 53, 107, 111

General Assembly of the United Nations, 8, 12, 16, 94, 109

Goitre, 49, 63-4

Government expenditures (table), 117

Ground nut flour, (see peanut flour)

Handicapped children, 26

Health, 19 ff.; education in, 20, 25 ff.; organization of services, 21-3; present extent of services, 20 ff.; programs to extend services, 23-4; services in India, 22-3; UNICEF aid to, 23-4, 26; WHO aid to, 26

High-protein foods, commercial production of, 69-70; research and development, 64-5; scientific considerations, 65-6

Hospitals, 22, 25

Housing, 17, 90

Human resources, investment in, 1 ff., 9-11; waste of, 5

Immunization, 20
Incaparina, 68
Income, 102-3
Industry, 8; lack of development of, 51
Inhabitants per physician (table), 21
Institute of Nutrition of Central America and Panama (INCAP), 49, 67
Institutions, residential, 92
International Labour Organisation (ILO), 79, 80, 81 ff., 96
International Union for Child Welfare, 109
Intestinal parasites, 29, 50
Iodized salt, 63-4
Isoniazid, 39

Kwashiorkor, 48, 49, 68

Leprosy, 10, 27, 29, 36 ff.; UNICEF aid to control of, 38
Lewis, W. A., 75

Malaria, 20, 27, 29, 30 ff.; eradication of, in Mexico, 32; UNICEF aid to eradication of, 31, 32; US aid to eradication of, 31; WHO eradication programs, 31
Malnutrition, 3, 10, 20, 45, 48, 52; natural history of, 46 ff.
Marasmus, 48
Matching, 100-1
Maternal and child health, centers, 22, 27; services, 5, 14, 109
Measles, 29
Milk, 47; breast milk, 47; conservation projects, UNICEF aid to, 58-9; dry milk distribution, 59 ff.; industrial processing of, 57; pasteurization of, 57, 58; sterilization of, 57, 58; world production of, 57
Molluscicides, 42
Mortality, among infants, 19; among pre-school children, 20; among school children, 20

National income, of developed countries, 2; of developing countries, 2
National planning and the needs of children, 13 ff.
National UNICEF committees, 111
Non-governmental organizations, 109 ff.
Nutrition, 45 ff.; applied, 62-3; education in, 61-2; fact-finding and planning, 54-6; of pre-school children, 5; surveys, 53-5; UNICEF assistance in the field of, 54
Nutritional disorders of children, 48-50

Oil-seed press-cakes, 64, 68

Parasitic infestation, 20, 24
Peanut flour, 69
Penicillin, 33
Personnel, shortages of, 4 ff., 10; in social services, 90; stages of attrition in development of (chart), 6
Planning, national, 13 ff.

Population, age distribution of, 10; growth of, in large cities (table), 85; increased population and food production, 52; problem, 3-4; rate of growth of, 3 ff.
Premature infants, 26
Primary school, education, 5; enrollment in, 72; expansion of, 5
Program priorities, establishment of, 97, 100
Projects, assisted by UNICEF (table), 118-19; implementation of, 102
Protective foods, 49, 57, 64; increased production of, 60 ff.
Protein Advisory Group, 65, 69, 97
Protein-calorie malnutrition, 45-6, 48
Protein-rich foods, 64-70

Red palm oil, 62
Resources, for children's services, 11-13; internal resources of developing countries, 11; from outside, 11-12; scarcity of, 1
Respiratory infections, 20, 29
Rickets, 49
Rockefeller Foundation, 65
Rural community development, 56-7, 89, 90

Saridele, 67, 68
Schistosoma parasites, 41, 42
School enrolment, by level (table), 72; per 10,000 population (chart), 73
School leavers, 74
Scrimshaw, Nevin, 49
Secondary school, education, 5; enrolment in, 72
Self-sustaining economic growth, 2, 11
Sen, B. R., 45, 53
Skim milk powder, 59 ff.; Canadian Government donation of, 59; distribution of, through MCH centers, 59; UNICEF distribution of, 59-60; US Government donation of, 59; vitamin A and D fortification, 60
Social change, 83; in rural areas, 84; in tropical Africa, 84-5; and urban growth, 85-7
Social services, 89 ff., 109; extension of, 89-90; primary aims of, 89
Soy, flours, 68; milks, 67; processing of, 67
Sulfone drugs, 37
Supplies and equipment shipped by UNICEF (table), 122-4
Syphilis, 33 ff.

Teaching, in developing countries, 74
Thailand, number of doctors in, 27; national health program, 27-8; UNICEF aid to, 28; US aid to, 28; WHO aid to, 28
The Needs of Children, 16-17, 94
Trachoma, 10, 20, 29, 35-6; UNICEF aid to campaigns against, 36; virus, 36
Traditional social institutions, breakdown of, 84-5

130